MARINE SCOUT SNIPERS

MARINE SCOUT SNIPERS

True Stories from U.S. Marine Corps Snipers

Lena Sisco

Guilford, Connecticut

An imprint of Rowman & Littlefield

Distributed by NATIONAL BOOK NETWORK

British Library Cataloguing in Publication Information Available

Library of Congress Cataloging-in-Publication Data

Names: Sisco, Lena, author.
Title: Marine scout snipers : true stories from U.S. Marine Corps snipers / Lena Sisco.
Other titles: True stories from U.S. Marine Corps snipers
Description: Guilford, Connecticut : Lyons Press, [2016]
Identifiers: LCCN 2016006417 (print) | LCCN 2016006608 (ebook) | ISBN 9781493018574 (pbk. : alk. paper) | ISBN 9781493026852 (electronic)
Subjects: LCSH: Snipers—United States—Interviews. | United States. Marine Corps—Commando troops—Biography. | Iraq War, 2003-2011—Personal narratives, American. | Afghan War, 2001—-Personal narratives, American.
Classification: LCC UD333 .S57 2016 (print) | LCC UD333 (ebook) | DDC 956.7044/3450922—dc23
LC record available at https://lccn.loc.gov/2016006417

Printed in the United States of America

CONTENTS

DEDICATION

This book is dedicated to the seven men who shared their combat experience as Marine Corps Scout Snipers with me so that I could share their stories with you. I want to thank them for volunteering to be a part of this project, and I want to thank them for their service and their commitment to keeping our nation safe. I also want to honor their families, who supported these men as they left behind wives, children, mothers, fathers, and siblings while they deployed to the front lines, not knowing if they would ever return. Ambition, motivation, and patriotism drove all of these men to become Marine Corps Scout Snipers; perseverance, professionalism, and loyalty got them back home safely.

Semper fi, short for "semper fidelis," has been the Marine Corps' motto since 1883. It is Latin for "always faithful," or "always loyal." It signifies the dedication and loyalty that each individual Marine has to the Corps and to their country. This loyalty extends even after Marines leave service. If you dare call a retired or honorably discharged Marine a "former Marine," be advised, you will be corrected. There are no "former" Marines; there are only Marines. Unlike other services, once a Marine, always a Marine. In the Navy, the Marine Corps' sister service, we have a saying, "fair winds and following seas." It is a nautical blessing when we toast farewell to friends. Although the origin is a bit of a mystery, it has to do with wishing another sailor safe journeys; fair winds and following seas are the ideal conditions when under way. So in essence we are wishing for the safety and well-being of others when we depart them. With that said, I would like to express my deepest gratitude to these seven Marines and bid you all *fair winds and following seas.*

ACKNOWLEDGMENTS

It goes without saying that the first individuals I want to express my sincerest gratitude to are those you will read about within the pages of this book: Mike Carr, Dave Hodulich, Sonny, Timothy La Sage, Fritz, and Zane, and one Marine who needs to remain anonymous. Your patience and dedication to this publication will never go without my humble and unrelenting appreciation. I want to thank you not only for dedicating the time out of your busy lives to work with me, but for your service in the United States Marine Corps. Too often you go forgotten. I would also like to acknowledge and honor your families and friends who stood by you while you served your country and the Corps, those who stayed at home having to live their lives and take over immense responsibilities while they waited for your safe return.

I want to thank Rory Compton and Nic Smith, who networked me to this amazing group of men.

A special thank-you to Lyons Press and my editor Eugene Brissie, production editor Alden Perkins and copyeditor Kathy Dvorsky, and Maryann Karinch, my agent.

And lastly, thank you to all of my family and friends who provided me encouraging words to keep driving on.

All of my best to you,
Lena

PREFACE

"Can we meet at Starbucks? I'd like to talk to you in person to get a feel for who you are and what your angle is before I agree to do this." This is what a Marine Corps Scout Sniper told me when a common acquaintance put me in touch with him and I asked him if he or any snipers he knew would like to be a part of this publication. He had to vet me first, understandably. I arrived at Starbucks about 4 o'clock on a windy Sunday knowing only the name of the individual I was supposed to meet: Rory. As I opened the door with my windblown Medusa hair, my MacBook Air tucked under my arm, my huge Coach diaper/ computer bag that I use as a purse on the other arm, and cell phone in hand, this young guy immediately caught my eye. He was watching me. *Was that Rory?* If it was, he looked exactly like Jake Gyllenhaal. "Are you Lena?" My question was answered. My first thought was that this couldn't be the sniper I was supposed to meet; he was way too clean-cut and young. In my mind I was picturing an older guy with facial hair, a bit rough around the edges, some tattoos maybe, in a plaid shirt—you know the type. Yes, I know, I hate to admit that I stereotyped. He stood up; we shook hands and exchanged pleasantries, and then we both sat down and he began to grill me, professionally and politely. He asked me why I was writing this book and what my angle was. I told him I was asked to write it. My agent contacted me and said a publishing company had asked her if she knew anyone that could write a book on snipers to dovetail with the release of the movie *American Sniper*. She immediately thought of me because I had just written a book with her and she knew I still had a lot of contacts within the military community, being a former military member myself; she also knows I love to write. She said the book would be a collection of stories from snipers that I would interview. Apparently the movie *American Sniper* drummed up some bad press and cast a negative shadow on the sniper community and the U.S. military in general; not the first time that's been done. I wasn't sure I was up to the challenge, but I thought about a personal experience I had years ago when I was in the military, and so the next day I called her and told her yes.

In 1997 I enlisted in the Navy Reserve. In 1999 I was certified as a Department of Defense Military Interrogator, and in 2000 I was commissioned as a Navy Reserve Intelligence Officer. Less than a year after 9/11, I was stationed at the detention camp in Guantanamo (GTMO) Bay, Cuba, to interrogate members of al-Qaeda and Taliban. Whenever people found out that I was an interrogator in GTMO, they would ask me, "Did you torture detainees there?" and each time I would reply, "No." But that's not what the news said. Unbeknownst to me, interrogators in GTMO allegedly waterboarded the detainees. Google *GTMO* and I bet you will see a ton of articles in which the writers vehemently claim that the U.S. tortured GTMO detainees. This baffles me, and it also angers me. I can't speak to what happened in Abu Ghraib in Iraq or what the CIA did at their notorious "black sites," but I can speak to what happened in GTMO from August 2002 to December 2002, and that is this: no military interrogator tortured detainees. I was there, and I worked in that prison. Yet it's in the media, so it must be true, right? Wrong. Almost seven years after that deployment I was subpoenaed as a prosecution witness for a military tribunal and had to return to GTMO. Reporters were swarming the island and the courtroom when I took the stand. Within minutes of my leaving the stand, "breaking news" from the courtroom would hit the World Wide Web. The reputable reporters would quote me verbatim, while the disreputable ones would make demeaning comments and report flat-out lies. It reminded of those celebrity gossip magazines; some people get off on other people's humiliation. In one particular article written by a degrading columnist who knew nothing about me, not even my name or identity, or GTMO, I was called a MILF (if you don't know what that is, it means "Mother I'd Like to [explicit])," insinuating how I was able to get information from one detainee. Professional, *right*? My mother had to read this about me. The irony of the situation is that just last year, 2014, I got a call from that same columnist, who wanted information from me about another interrogator I assume he wanted to slander too, who was also stationed in GTMO back in the day. He had no idea he had just called the person he called a MILF years prior. I laughed to myself and, of course, never returned his phone call. My point in sharing that story is this: do not believe everything you read online or see on TV. Seek a second opinion. This book is your second opinion; in reality, it's the truth to the accusations about military snipers. I hope to refute the negative stereotype that *American Sniper* has stirred up about military snipers. This book is a collection of firsthand accounts of combat missions provided by the people who were there in battle, Marine Corps Scout Snipers. Believe what these snipers share with you about what it's like to live during this time as we continually struggle to thwart terrorism. I was asked to write this book, and I accepted because my intent is to get the raw stories, the truth, out to the general public. A question we should ask ourselves is, how do military snipers feel when they have to hear the criticism that defames their pride, honor, and courage—their job?

I can't take back the lies that were written specifically about me, and I don't care, because that was a long time ago. But what I can do today is provide readers with accurate accounts of what it's like to be a sniper: the arduous training, the heartbreak of leaving family behind, the adrenaline of deploying to a war zone, the emotional burden of operational mistakes, the pain of having to bury your friends who died next to you in combat, the gratification of killing the enemy, and the anxiety of being hunted by the enemy.

Rory warmed up to me, and as we departed Starbucks, he said, "I'll get you some guys." The next day my phone was blowing up with text messages from guys saying they heard I needed snipers for a book I was writing and they were interested in being interviewed. I guessed I'd passed Rory's vetting process; thank you, Rory! In fact, one day I was texting a sniper, Dave, whom I only ever communicated with via text and email (which is terrible, I know, especially being an interpersonal communications expert). Apparently my voice to text incorrectly trans-lated *Dave* to "babe," which he took rather well, but it made me very em-barrassed. He joked that I was calling him "babe" and he had never even seen me! So I asked him jokingly, "You didn't Google me to validate my credentials?" He replied, "I had another Scout Sniper tell me you were the real deal, so that was all I needed to hear." That put a smile on my face. And meeting all of them and hearing their stories just solidified the sense of brotherhood they have among themselves. That is a special thing. I can share Dave's name and the names of some of the other snipers, but I have changed the other names for reasons of security and to protect their privacy. I didn't change much of their prose because I wanted it to reflect their personalities. I shared some of my personal experiences and some historical data within their stories, but most of what you will read comes straight from their mouths. I think what I enjoyed most about this project was seeing and hearing their humble pride as I interviewed them and listened to their fantastic achievements. For what they lived through, they all deserve to have an ego, but I couldn't find a hint of it in any one of them. Here's a look into the lives of Marine Corps Scout Snipers. I hope their stories will enlighten, entertain, and educate you.

INTRODUCTION

The movie *American Sniper*, directed by Clint Eastwood, is about a U.S. Navy SEAL sniper named Chris Kyle (played by actor Bradley Cooper) and came out in theaters on December 25, 2014. With it came a flurry of controversy, ranging from critics condemning it as war propaganda to advocates praising it as the first accurate war movie. Among the critics was Michael Moore, an American director, producer, writer, and liberal political activist, who, when expressing his opinion about the movie, called snipers "cowards." Moore later praised the film but still stated, "I think most Americans don't think snipers are heroes." It's unclear as to whether or not he included himself in the group of "most Americans"; even so, I would hope Moore regretted making that comment immediately after he said it for obvious reasons, and also because he should know that he can't, nor shouldn't, speak for *most* Americans. But if he feels that way, my only guess as to why would be because snipers are usually engaging the enemy from concealed positions; "from the hide." So perhaps he thinks snipers are "hiding" while targeting the enemy instead of running up against them the way you see it in movies using computer-generated imagery to depict epic battles; *The Lord of the Rings* and *300* come to mind. How could a sniper fire at the enemy without exposing his position and getting shot and killed in return if he wasn't concealed? That's exactly why we have snipers: so they can stay concealed to take out the enemy threat while protecting the movement of our other forces within an area of operation. Snipers are most certainly *not* cowards. They are the ones who have to get closer to enemy positions than anyone else, without immediate firepower nearby backing them up. They are usually in a four-man team, sanitized (meaning no identification on them), hiding out for days with only the food, water, ammunition, and equipment they have on their backs. If the situation gets bad, they have to call in air support, making sure the gunships don't accidentally target them. I like to think of snipers as silent warriors; they have to be stealthy to be able to get as close as they do to observe the enemy, take out the enemy, and stay concealed so they don't become the enemy's kills.

Another critic of the film said *American Sniper* was "disgusting" and that the character Bradley Cooper played just enjoyed killing people and bragging about it. Another said it should be a "satire about a redneck killer who killed hundreds of people because of a terror attack against his country he saw on TV." The last part of that comment struck a chord with me; it almost sounds like the critic is downplaying the attack against the United States because the character didn't personally experience the attack—he just "watched it on TV." Well, a lot of Americans *just* watched 9/11 on TV and still felt the anguish of what was happening on American soil. I saw that same terror attack on TV with Matt Lauer and Katie Couric while on a ten-minute break from my officer etiquette class when I was attending a Naval Officer Direct Commission school. I went on to help fight against the terrorists who attacked the country I live in in my own way, as a military interrogator, even though I wasn't in New York City at the time experiencing it firsthand. I don't understand how seeing the attack on TV lessens the fact that our country was attacked by terrorists, and thousands of innocent people died that day. Those who weren't killed have to live with the emotional and physical aftermath of that horrendous day. Another review said, "We should be compassionate and put ourselves in other people's shoes in order to protect the U.S." While I agree 100 percent that the world needs more compassion, we also need to realize that those "shoes" are the shoes of extremists who hate everything we stand for and have no compassion themselves; they have passion for taking nonbelievers' lives, but not compassion for life. And if you haven't met them face-to-face like I have and heard it from them, you'll never understand this. It's very difficult, almost impossible, to have compassion for people who want to kill you just for being born American. I have an anthropology/ archaeology background and graduated from one of the most liberal-minded universities in the United States; then I joined the military and became an interrogator. That was the best school I have ever attended; I got an amazing education, and joining the military was one of the best decisions I ever made. I don't separate the two: both have positively influenced my life, but I have met people who think you have to be one or the other. Either you are a liberal academic, or you are a conservative joining the military; I happen to be both and proud of each. My unique background and experiences let me view military operations through a different lens, which led to numerous successes as an interrogator in GTMO. I used rapport, compassion, and empathy to build trust and respect with hard-core terrorists; of course, along with my questioning, elicitation, and deception-detecting techniques. I didn't try to change their beliefs; I just listened to them and offered respect, even though they disgusted me. But at the end of the day, I couldn't change their thinking, and so I didn't try. In fact, one detainee told me, "I like you, but you must realize, if I see you on the street when I get out of here, I have to kill you." Acceptance of letting them have their fanatical ideals allowed me to gather a lot of intelligence information. I like to think that I have compassion for people and for their ways of life. It would be great if ethnocentrism didn't exist and there was better acceptance for other cultures. Nevertheless, I have learned that you can't change a culture in a year, a decade, or during a war campaign, plain and simple—especially when that culture has leaders who fuel their hatred and discontent. And if a group of people wants to kill the group of people I am a part of (Americans) out of ignorance, extremism, lack of compassion, passion, values, and beliefs then I am all for fighting fire with fire. Our military snipers are not "people haters" or "killers." They are protecting people and saving lives; that's war, and that's why we have a military to either capture or exterminate threats against our nation.

The United States has conducted psychological operations (PSYOPS) for "winning the hearts and minds" in Iraq and Afghanistan. This campaign works with the Iraqis and Afghans who are not extremists. But we are fighting extremists. There is no reasoning with extremists. Trust me, I tried. They have deep-seated beliefs that go back for centuries. In fact, many of the detainees who were released from GTMO have gone back to the front lines to fight against us again, even though they were apparently "reformed."

Here is a classic example of a group of extremists and rebel fighters who received compassion from a capturing force. The capturers let them surrender to retreat back to their home countries, but the extremists slighted that compassion, meeting it with force instead. Do you remember the events that happened in Afghanistan right after the 9/11 terrorist attacks? In November 2001 the Taliban field commanders agreed to surrender their forces to General Abdul Rashid Dostum's forces, the Northern Alliance, outside the city of Kunduz, Afghanistan. Hundreds of Afghan Taliban members and foreign fighters (non-Afghans) surrendered their weapons and were loaded onto trucks near Kunduz. Some were taken to Sheberghan Prison and some were taken to the Qala-i-jangi fortress near the city Mazar-i-Sharif to be questioned about affiliations with al-Qaeda. Qala-i-jangi was an old fortress that Dostum used as his headquarters and ammunitions depot. For those of you who don't know the story, you can already sense the setup for disaster. Although these men agreed to surrender to the Northern Alliance, some of them had kept grenades hidden on their persons even after being told to surrender all weapons and after being searched. While at Qala-i-jangi during the searching process, one of the prisoners revolted and pulled the pin on a grenade he had concealed in his clothing, killing himself and a Northern Alliance soldier. Then another prisoner pulled the pin on his grenade, and it exploded, killing him and some others nearby. The two incidents led to a chain reaction of unforeseen events. Chaos ensued, and soon the other prisoners, numbering in the hundreds, decided to revolt against the Northern Alliance soldiers instead of surrender. They ultimately waged a full-on uprising and began attacking the two Americans (CIA) who were conducting the questioning, killing one of them. The prisoners soon gained control on the ground and then gained access to the ammunitions depot. What was supposed to be a peaceful surrender turned into a three-day, bloody battle. General Dostum had compassion for their lives—at first. When he initially met with the Taliban commanders who agreed that their people would surrender, Dostum told the Taliban commanders he was going to let all the fighters go back home with no repercussions; he was wiping the slate clean. But his compassion was met with retaliation. A lot of men lost their lives during those three days. Why? Because the inherent nature of those men, influenced by the culture in which they existed, was to fight for what they believed in and against what they hated, not to be compassionate about human life. One of my detainees told me about that day, as he was one of the eighty or so survivors who was sent to GTMO and ended up sitting across the table from me. So, you see, you can't change a culture or expect people to agree with our beliefs. In order for compassion to protect the United States, it has to exist on both sides of the fence, with us and with our enemies. One day that may happen in a perfect world, but I'm not holding my breath for that day, because the world and all of the people who inhabit it are not perfect and will never be.

In 2012 I trained members of the Marine Corps operational forces. During this training I ran an exercise that involved Marines manning checkpoints in high-threat environments where they were required to screen local nationals to obtain information regarding the security situation of the area and to determine if enemy forces were nearby. Even though we tried to create a training environment that would closely replicate the real world, we couldn't simulate the threat of enemy snipers: a critical security risk down range in real-world operations. Enemy snipers are a huge threat to the security of our forces forward deployed. They assist in ambushing our convoys, they target our key personnel, they hunt our snipers, and they thwart movement of our forces. The enemy has snipers, and the U.S. snipers protect our forward-deployed forces from them.

Our military snipers undergo specialized training and operate independently with little support from their parent commands. Snipers are chosen based on their marksmanship, mental stability, patience, and physical ability. They stalk the enemy while concealed in their operational overwatches, to protect our checkpoints, convoys, and direct-action missions. They also seek out the enemy snipers. Their lives are not lives of glory and fame; their lives are filled with sacrifices and hardships for which they are most often not even thanked or recognized. It's about training until you are sleep deprived and having to do your job successfully every time, because the consequences of not being successful could be loss of innocent lives, or living with consequences that could haunt you till the day you die. In the end, they are service members, and just like any other service member they are defending the country they live in by putting their lives on the line, willingly.

This book is a collection of stories from Marine Corps Scout Snipers who have deployed overseas in high-threat environments; the stories involve their experiences at the unclassified level. These are real people and real stories. You will get a glimpse of the cold reality of what it's like to be in their shoes, overseas, in a foreign country on unfamiliar land, away from families and any sense of normalcy, being hunted by an enemy who hates everything they stand for. You will get a sense of the camaraderie between sniper team members and the sacrifices they make for each other, for the military, for their country, and for their families. They sacrifice willingly, knowing that with one perfect shot from enemy fire they may not be going back home to their country, their family, their kids, their pets, their lives. You will learn to empathize with them as others berate them in the press for promoting killing; and these are the very same people the snipers are indirectly protecting. You will see how one split-second decision could have changed their fate for eternity. These snipers will share with you how it feels to actually kill another human being, and how that affects them years on in life. You will read about their training and tactics and their professionalism, and you will feel the stress they endure, from training to combat, to returning home and trying to assimilate back into everyday life. This book is not a Hollywood account of supercharged action figures and fast-paced stories with high crescendos; this book is a collection of real-world stories from Marine Corps scout snipers, including the monotonous life of deployment while waiting for a combat mission, the tedious analysis work while on post, the mistakes that they can't take back, and of course, their kills.

You will be taken on journeys to the most destitute environments as you read about their missions. You will learn how they use their mastery of sniper skills to mitigate threats and negate the enemy's ability to disrupt U.S. operations. You will feel the anxiety of their operational tempo, and you will hear their successes and failures, their struggles and their lessons learned. You will also know what it feels like to live with a group of men in a small, confined area, with just the bare essentials, day in and day out, and how they protect each other during combat. You'll get a look into the weapons, gear, and equipment they use, as well as their collateral duties and responsibilities outside of expert shooting skills. You will see how conventional forces treat them, how they are sometimes praised, sometimes disgraced. Finally, you will get to meet the people behind the rifles as they share their personal stories. These are anonymous heroes who pass us by in parks; who shop in the same supermarkets we do; who are homeowners, fathers, and brothers; who worry about paying bills, just like us. What is different, though, is that when they go to work, they don't put in an eight-hour day with a one-hour lunch. There is no leaving early on Friday for happy hour or to start a long holiday weekend. There is no room for picking up the slack another day. There is no going home to wind down over a hot meal and a beer. When they are working, they have to be at the top of their game every day, and every minute of that day. And there is always that chance they won't be coming home after work.

I want to share one more review with you. It was by Jon Davis, a Marine Corps Marksman Instructor, titled "A Former Marine's Review of *American Sniper*," on February 9, 2015 (http://time.com/3699063/ marines-review-american-sniper/). He wrote about something I experienced while deployed in GTMO, something I am not proud to admit to or say, especially with my academic background. He wrote this:

> When I sat down for the movie I fully expected all the nonsense and war drama that was *The Hurt Locker*. My only hope was that Clint Eastwood, whose work I have enjoyed in the past, would do better. The lights went down and the opening began to the Islamic call to prayer. Before even the first frame of actual film footage, I was shocked that I was immediately back to that other time and place. What the Adhan means, to me, is an immediate sense of anxiety and foreboding. I know that for billions of people, that is not the truth, but when the first place you hear it is over hundreds of loudspeakers echoing from the village of Haditha below your base, it is more reminiscent of the people living there lobbing rockets at you every week than of any religion of peace.

I heard the call to prayer, the *adhan*, playing over the loudspeakers in the detention camp every day, multiple times a day, when I was stationed at GTMO. We played it to honor the detainees' religious beliefs and to allow them to practice their religion in the detention camp. I often allowed my detainees to pray in peace and quiet in the interrogation booth, after the guards escorted to them to the head (bathroom) so they could wash for prayer. However, when I hear the adhan today, I can't help but feel a slight pang of an ill feeling, perhaps anger, perhaps remorse, perhaps fear. When I saw Indiana Jones as a teenager, all I wanted to be was a female version of him. I wanted to be an archaeologist and travel the globe for adventure. I wanted to see "giant vampire bats" in India (of course, there is no such thing—those were fruit bats in the movie *Indiana Jones and the Temple of Doom*), and I wanted to walk through street markets in Cairo. (Today you can't even travel to Egypt because of the threat of terrorism, which is very disheartening.) Although I did become an archaeologist, I never had those types of adventures. Regardless, the Middle East was this romantic place to me, with the bazaars, music, and majestic architecture. Back then the adhan added to the allure. Unfortunately, after my time spent in GTMO during the Global War on Terror (GWOT), when I hear that sound I am immediately taken back to that detention camp. I hate that that is my initial reaction and feeling, but I worked in a prison with hundreds of detainees who mostly practiced Islam (ironic, since Islam is all about peace—I guess the extremists missed that message). They would tell me they would kill me the first chance they got and that the U.S. deserved 9/11; they would then try to commit suicide on a daily basis so that the "brothers" would come attack the U.S. again. The sound of the adhan becomes a haunting reminder of the hatred of the inmates inside it, and the fear of more terrorist attacks. Please don't think I am ignorant enough to think every Muslim is associated with terrorism; that is ridiculous. It would be like saying every Catholic is associated with Opus Dei (the extreme wing of Catholicism). But I, and a lot of other people I know who served in GWOT, can relate to Mr. Davis's feelings of anxiety and foreboding, as we are also quickly taken back to an unpleasant time. I still long for the day to visit Morocco and Egypt, and maybe then when I hear the call to prayer in a new environment, I will finally enjoy it again. And I hope the terrorists have some thread of decency to protect these countries' cultural history; but I know they don't.

Mr. Davis goes on to praise the film for its degree of accurate details and even said, "Bradley Cooper got it right." Most war veterans keep our unpleasant memories and emotions associated with those memories hidden, or at least only discuss them with other military members. They aren't talked about for many reasons; no one will know what it's really like to have gone through what they did, so trying to explain sometimes does no good; in fact, it can cause more frustration. They also aren't allowed to talk about most of those unpleasant memories for security and classification reasons, and why would they want to burden someone else with those memories anyway? Any military member can tell you it's easier just to compartmentalize those feelings and memories instead of sharing them with outsiders. It is very hard to put yourself in the shoes of our service members. I can't even do it always, and I was a service member. I was never shot at nor had people dying around me, so I'll never understand the emotions associated with that. I can sympathize, but I will never know how they truly feel or the nightmares they endure. I'll never know what it's like to be able to sleep for only two hours at a time because you're worried about the next rocket attack.

You are entitled to form your own opinions about snipers, but before you do, I want to give you accurate information to do so. I hope you won't be easily persuaded by what you read and hear in the news, or watch in a Hollywood film. You may read about things like operational decisions you don't agree with, but try to put yourselves in their combat boots. I hope these stories provide you with a deeper insight to the personal and professional life of a sniper. I hope you'll see these men for what they really are: heroes versus cowards, and professionals versus "killers."

1

"THE THRILL ISN'T THE KILL, IT'S SURVIVING THE GAME"

WHAT IT'S REALLY LIKE TO BE A U.S. MARINE CORPS CHIEF SCOUT SNIPER

We are professionals. This is our job; we're not killers. We have to be jacks-of-all-trades. There were no specialists back in the day when I was deployed. We did it all. When you are limited with only three or four of us in a sniper team, you do everything. For me, I liked sneaking in, getting eyes on target, gathering and reporting information, and getting out without them knowing I was even there. I know some of my buddies would rather assault a defense or be in an attack, but for me it was more challenging and exciting remaining undetected. I want people to know that being a sniper was sometimes more about reporting what I saw back "to the rear" than taking a shot. Being a sniper involves tedious preparatory work, analysis, concentration, and observation skills. Don't get me wrong: we spend a lot of hours on the range and in the classroom to master and maintain our proficiency to hit a target out to one thousand yards. But we also have to work on our patience, paying attention to details and staying focused when it is cold, wet, and dark, having been up for hours, patrolling with 120-pound packs for miles, until you're on the objective. And then after all of that, you're still required to perform your best. It takes discipline to stay awake and not miss any action or detail, especially during those long hours of pure boredom in the heat while you are drenched in sweat. But to me, it was all worth it, every minute of it. Why am I providing my story? I want people to know it takes a lot to do this job; it's not about being an action hero, and it comes with a price to pay.

Here is Mike's story. He will take you to Haiti, Somalia, and Afghanistan. Sometimes you will be on the edge of your seat like he was, and other times you will feel the monotonous, mundane days drag on, like he did.

1993/HAITI (OPERATION PROVIDE DEMOCRACY): THE CLOSE CALL

In April 1993 Mike attended the ten-week 2nd Marine Division Scout Sniper School at Marine Corps Base Camp Lejeune, North Carolina, that trained him to become a Marine Scout Sniper, which awarded him the MOS (Military Occupational Specialty) of "8541." Camp Lejeune is one of the Marine Corps training bases and is called the "home of expeditionary forces in readiness." He learned a wide variety of skills to include shooting stationary and moving targets out to one thousand yards, stalking, mission planning, land navigation, patrolling, sketching, communications, use of supporting arms, and reporting. After Mike's training, tensions on the Caribbean island of Haiti had escalated when the democratically elected Haitian President, Jean-Bertrand Aristide, was overthrown by a faction of Haiti's military regime. Upon hearing that Haiti's military regime had forcibly occupied the government and overthrown Aristide, U.S. forces began operational planning for restoring the government to its people. Armed forces assembled and staged in southern Florida, Puerto Rico, Hunter Army Airfield in Savannah, Georgia, and in Guantanamo Bay, Cuba, preparing to invade Haiti. By October 1993, a rifle company, Mike and his sniper platoon, part of Headquarters and Service Company (part of the 2/8 Battalion), and some headquarters staff of the 2/8 Battalion were issued orders to deploy off the coast of Haiti in support of Operation Provide Democracy. This was different from Operation Uphold Democracy, but it occurred at the same time. The distinction between the two was that the entire battalion did not deploy for Provide Democracy, just the smaller element Mike was in, which was sent to assist with the evacuation of U.S.

personnel if it came to that. Mike's mission was to provide security to U.S. forces while they set up defenses on a pier at the Port-au-Prince port facility, which was designated as the access pier for U.S. ships coming to support the operation.

Anyone who has been trained in or involved in real-world operational planning knows that typically the mission is defined first, and then plans to accomplish the mission are designed. These operational plans (OPLANs), also called courses of action, or COAs, usually come in threes, and the best of the three COAs is selected for the mission. The crises in Haiti resulted in three COAs/OPLANs. The first dealt with a total force invasion from the land and sea if the U.S. was not allowed to enter Haiti with permission. The second dealt with a permissive entry still with large numbers of troops who were combat ready. The third fell somewhere in between the first two while still maintaining offensive capabilities. The U.S. simultaneously strategized for two of the OPLANs in order to set foot in Haiti to help restore the regime. One of the plans, Operation Uphold Democracy, would take effect if the U.S. was allowed to enter Haiti, and the other plan, Operation Restore Democracy, would take effect if the U.S. had to enter Haiti forcibly. Talks and negotiations supervened. The military regime, although saying they would relinquish authority back to Aristide, did not, and they continued to rule over Haiti's deteriorating economy. Living conditions were becoming so oppressive in Haiti that thousands of impoverished Haitians were fleeing the country and attempting to illegally enter the United States. The U.S. had two objectives back then: get Aristide back in power and reduce the flow of illegal immigrants into the United States.

Mike was set to assume the position of platoon sergeant for this mission because the Marine who was the actual platoon sergeant had broken his foot and couldn't deploy. A few days prior to their scheduled departure from CONUS (continental United States), Mike's platoon sergeant (we'll call him Staff Sergeant F) asked him if he would consider leading a sniper team instead of deploying in place of him as a platoon sergeant. At the time Mike was serving as the chief scout, which is the senior school-trained sniper in the platoon. (As the chief scout, he would automatically assume the role of platoon sergeant if the actual platoon sergeant was unavailable anyway.) Mike was prepared to assume that role especially since he had just deployed to Mountain Warfare Training Center in

Bridgeport, California, as a platoon sergeant during training and workups (military slang for a period of training and preparations before deployment). He had become tightly knit with the platoon members and was eager to serve in a leadership role. Taking on the responsibilities of this position for a deployment would be a great experience, and even though it would also be a great bullet on his FITREP (fitness report), he didn't care about that; it was all about taking care of the Marines.

Not having made his decision yet while still at Camp Lejeune prior to deployment, Staff Sergeant F had been hearing some rumblings from sniper team members about their apprehension and worry regarding their current team leader. They told Staff Sergeant F that their team leader didn't have the skills or experience to lead them in combat; he had no real-world experience leading a sniper team, and he had only been to sniper training school, with no experience in a four-man scout sniper team. They were about to embark on a real-world operation, and there was no room for mistakes. You can't start over like you can in training. Mike had already been deployed to northern Iraq in 1991 as part of a rifle company for Operation Provide Comfort and to Okinawa and Korea on a Unit Deployment Program (a system for assigning deployments for the Marine Corps) with the same sniper platoon conducting training and bilateral training with the Republic of Korea (ROK) Marines in 1992. As a result, Staff Sergeant F thought it would be a better fit to have Mike deploy as their team leader instead. If any Marine, soldier, sailor, or airman has trust and confidence issues with their leaders, this is a setup for disaster when down range (a term the military uses when deploying OCONUS [outside the continental United States]). Not only does it negatively affect morale, but while deployed in a hostile environment, whether in combat or not, you have enough stress from the high-tempo environment and trying to keep yourself and others safe that the last thing you need to worry about is having an inept leader responsible for your well-being; you need that extra sense of security that comes from trusting your leaders. Mike was faced with a choice: should he lead an entire platoon on deployment, or should he give that sniper team a leader they could trust on their mission? Mike chose what his heart and mind told him to: he chose to lead the sniper team, and in early October 1993 he deployed off the coast of Haiti as a sniper team leader for Operation Provide Democracy. He flew from Camp Lejeune in North Carolina to Guantanamo Bay, Cuba, with the rifle company, some headquarters Marines, and the snipers. Once they landed in Guantanamo Bay, they boarded a ship that sailed to and was stationed off the coast of Haiti and were told to *stand by*. Mike was on the USS *Nassau* (LHA-4), a Tarawa-class amphibious assault ship, in the Caribbean Sea from October 18 until October 31, 1993. Every day he woke up on the ship wondering if the call would come that day. "I wasn't nervous; I was excited and focused. I had already done two six-month Landing Force 6th Fleet deployments on ships, so I was used to ship life at this point. On my first deployment we did contingency operations off the coast of Lebanon to rescue Colonel William R. Higgins and evacuate other Americans, and on my second deployment we went into northern Iraq for three months as part of a rifle company." Now Mike's sniper team conducted mission planning, rehearsals, and reconnaissance and surveillance (called R&S) both ashore at GITMO and while on board the ship as U.S. planning ensued for invasion.

I remember back in 1997, as part of my workups with the BLT 3/6, I was on the USS GUAM conducting SOCEX (Special Operations Capable Exercise Certifying our MEU [Marine Expeditionary Unit] to be certified Special Operations Capable). We received the warning order (notification of a pending mission) for a training mission ashore in the U.S. So we started mission planning to prepare to deploy as the reconnaissance and surveillance element. While doing this, we changed into civilian clothes since we would get off the helos at a civilian airport. A lot of the Marines kept saying, "You think you guys are so high speed because you are wearing civvies." We all just kept doing what we were doing. At one point I went to the hanger deck to inspect my team's gear. We had all of our individual gear and weapons (night-vision goggles, personal rifles, pistols, camouflage paint, MREs [which stands for meals ready-to-eat], etc.), we had the team gear (radios, reporting formats, sketch kits, field expedient antenna kits), and then any mission-specific gear, which was all laid out uniformly on our poncho liners. All the common gear was laid out in the same spot on each member's poncho liner with team- and mission-specific gear in the same spot on each poncho liner as well. I would go through and verify that each item was present and worked. I made sure the radio frequencies were correct and that we could talk to other radios. After the inspection was complete we all would pack our equipment. While this was going on, the other Marines (not in our platoon) seemed to change their tune about us being all "high-speed." I heard one of them

say, "Oh shit, that is professional. We don't do anything like that." Like I
said earlier, we are professionals and we are professional at what we do.

His mission for Operation Provide Democracy was to take his
team of two into Haiti with the rifle company (which was about 140
people), move to high ground, station at posts that overlooked the
pier below, and provide security cover while the rest of the company
conducted operations at the Port-au-Prince port. Just hours before the
U.S. planned to conduct a full-on invasion of Haiti, President Clinton
dispatched a team led by former President Jimmy Carter to try and ne-
gotiate with the de facto Haitian leadership. As a result, General Raoul
Cedras, head of the Haitian armed forces, signed a United Nations
Agreement on July 3, 1993, that called for the legitimate government
to be restored. On October 31 Aristide resumed his role as president.
Mike and his team were still on the USS *Nassau* waiting off the coast
as this took place. "We had a date planned to go in, but instead we got
all the ships, three I think, online and did a show of force by coming
over the horizon and stopping a few miles off the coast in plain view."
Mike's team never went ashore for two reasons: first, negotiations
were successful, and second, the U.S. had just lost eighteen soldiers
in Task Force Ranger in Mogadishu, Somalia. They were killed earlier
in the month. The national command authority didn't want to have
military casualties in two different theaters of operation in the same
month. In the end, the U.S. only had to demonstrate a show of force
with the ships coming from over the horizon into full view of the coast
of Haiti. It sent the message, "We mean business." Operation Provide
and Uphold Democracy had positive outcomes. The U.S. met both
of their objectives: to restore the democratically elected Aristide to
power and curtail illegal emigration, and our soldiers didn't have to
go into combat—a win-win situation for all. Although Mike didn't
see combat on this tour, his decision to lead the sniper team versus
the platoon still proved to be the right choice. He had concern for
the well-being of the Marines he was leading, and even though they
never went ashore, he was there for them and with them if they did.
A few days later he got word that he could leave the ship and return
back to Camp Lejeune. "I remember on the morning of the day I was
scheduled to leave the ship to go back stateside to assume orders to

FAST Company, the Navy personnel on board were pretty upset about something that happened the night before. It was Halloween, and apparently someone greased up in camo paint for mischief night and put their camo-painted hands all over the ladder rails in officer country. So when the officers touched the rails, they got the paint on their hands unknowingly and then touched their uniforms, getting camo paint all over them. The culprits were never caught." ("Officer country" on a ship refers where the officer quarters are located; you know this by the blue tile on the floor. If you have never been on a Navy ship, you have to use the handrails going up or down the ladders, or you'll end up on your back, or face first, on the deck below.)

While Operation Uphold Democracy planning continued, Mike was flown back to Camp Lejeune, where he would execute orders to Fleet Antiterrorism Security Team (FAST) Company in Norfolk.

Throughout his training while in the 2/8 Scout Sniper Platoon, FAST, and the Battalion Landing Team 3/6 Scout Sniper Platoon, Mike was learning something else other than honing his shooting skills and good leadership qualities. He was learning that outside of being an expert shooter, critical skills such as observation, reporting, and the use of supporting arms (which would be calling in mortars, artillery, and close air support [CAS]) were just as important to the success of the overall unit mission as taking a single successful shot. As he was taught, what they do as a four-man team can have huge impacts and implications for the battalion and beyond. "With one wrong shot, killing an innocent individual can have implications far beyond the battlefield. There are political and social implications, as well as personal, and you have to live with it." Yes, he was a highly trained weapons handler and could engage targets with his M40 out to one thousand yards, but as he states, "You have to remember, if I, or another team member, fired a direct fire weapon, that would clue the enemy that someone was in the area, and they would start searching for us. Maintaining concealment from the enemy to observe, report, and study their tactics, techniques, and procedures (what we call TTPs) is critical." He isn't concealed just to take out the enemy with his bullets; he's there to report on enemy locations and movements, to assess safe routes for friendly forces to use, and to stay undetected by the enemy, and you will see how this played a big part when he was deployed to Mogadishu, Somalia.

1994/MOGADISHU, SOMALIA (OPERATION RESTORE HOPE): CRITICAL OBSERVATION

Mike was initially designated to go to FAST Company back stateside to help teach sniping skills, but when he got there, the company commander had other plans for him. The commander thought Mike would benefit both personally and professionally from gaining a better understanding of the FAST mission support role by assigning him to the next platoon deploying to Somalia. While deployed to Somalia, Mike would learn the unique capabilities of a FAST Platoon, which included things like close quarter battle (CQB), armed convoy escort operations, high-risk personnel security, and personal specialized armament. The role of the FAST is to detect, deter, and defend against threats, with a focus on antiterrorism. FAST company platoons provide a limited-duration, expeditionary security force to protect vital naval and national assets. A common FAST Company mission is serving as security reinforcements at U.S. embassies around the world. FAST maintains forward-deployed platoons at various naval commands around the globe and is also based in the U.S., acting as alert forces capable of rapidly responding to unforeseen contingencies worldwide. Each FAST Company is equipped and trains with some of the most state-of-the-art weaponry. Unlike in an infantry platoon, in a fifty-man FAST Platoon every Marine is not only trained and qualified on a rifle and pistol, but they are also trained on the medium and heavy machine guns, MP-5, and shotguns. Only snipers and DMs (Designated Marksmen) are trained and equipped with designated marksman rifles (DMRs) and sniper rifles. The 0351s (MOS for Infantry Assaultman) are the only ones trained on SMAWs (shoulder-launched multipurpose assault weapons), and 0341s (MOS for Infantry Mortarman) are the only ones trained on M224 60mm mortars.

Although the FAST Platoon had all of this armament to bring with them to Somalia to help protect the U.S. embassy and all its personnel, the ambassador said they couldn't bring SMAW rockets or 60mm mortars into the country because they were too offensive in nature. The ambassador wanted to maintain the appearance of a more defensive posture than offensive. Even though his FAST platoon only wanted to bring in the mortars to fire illumination rounds to light up the area in front of embassy, they still weren't able to. Mike said this was a very typical scenario; "We would tell the ambassador, 'This is what we need to bring into the country to protect you,' and the response would be, 'You can't bring all that in here, and you can't set up there; it's my rose garden.' That's how it went."

In Somalia, FAST had been rotating platoons on four-month rotations to guard the U.S. embassy compound in Mogadishu and the ambassador while he traveled outside the compound. Mike was excited to deploy to Somalia versus staying stateside training, and it turned out to be a great career move for him. Mike deployed as a rifle squad leader with the FAST Platoon. Aside from his sniping duties, he had also been trained in CQB (room-clearing) combat fighting (engaging the enemy at close proximity, about thirty meters, with personal weapons), Enhanced Military Operations in urban terrain (combat conducted in urban areas such as towns and cities), and convoy operations (which involves planning, organizing, and conducting convoy movements). In addition, Mike attended basic Forward Observer (FO) courses in his last unit, where he learned how to call for fire with mortars and artillery as well as close air support. "Basically, you are the observer on the ground and call via radio to the mortar or artillery Fire Direction Center with coordinates to where you want them to have the mortar and artillery to land. Or in the case of CAS we acted as the terminal controller. Think 'JTAC' now, but this was before they termed it that. We would contact the pilot and give them coordinates to the enemy location and our location as well as any other friendly forces." JTAC stands for joint terminal attack controller and is the term used in the United States Armed Forces for a qualified military service member who, from a forward position, directs the action of combat aircraft engaged in close air support and other offensive air operations (http://www .military.com/video/operations-and-strategy/air-strikes/jtac-calling-in -air-strikes/2484564598001/). As part of the FAST Platoon's workup, U.S. Air Force personnel trained Mike, Sergeant T, and Captain B how to call for AC-130 gunship fire missions. "A lot of the Marines I keep in touch with today are from that time. I get messages to this day about how much of an effect I had on them back then; you'll see in a story I share at the end. It is very humbling!"

Prior to deploying to Somalia, during their CRE (which stands for Commanders Readiness Evaluation; it was an exercise where FAST would evaluate and certify the platoons who were ready for the deployment), Mike remembered a funny event that eased any concerns he had about who he would be deploying with. "It was the second night of the CRE, and we had been up for most of the last forty-eight hours. To try to get into our heads they would play music on a loop over and over again over a loudspeaker. The music they chose was Barney. I woke up about 0200 to Barney singing about peanut butter and jelly. I hear 'peanut, peanut butter and jelly' and as my eyes focus I see my Marines dancing around and waving an MRE peanut butter packet in one hand and a jelly packet in the other in sync to the music. I just started laughing. I knew this was a great bunch of guys and I would have no worries about us over in Somalia!"

The day came in mid-June 1994, when Captain B, Mike's platoon commander; Sergeant T, one of the other squad leaders in Mike's platoon; and Mike flew to Somalia as an advanced party (which means they arrived prior to the rest of the platoon) to the United States Liaison Office (USLO) in Mogadishu, Somalia.

> I know that to this day I still smell things and flash back to Mogadishu and the "shit shacks" outside the walls along the Dead Cow Road and south of Market Street. Shortly after the whole platoon arrived in Mogadishu we had an in-brief by the CI [counterintelligence] Marines there assigned to the USLO on the Task Force Ranger raid [which was the Battle of Mogadishu on October 3–4, 1993, commonly referred to as "Black Hawk Down," when two U.S. Black Hawks were shot down by rocket-propelled grenade launchers] and watched the footage from that day. We watched a forty-five-minute clip of the raid; the Black Hawk going down and how quickly they were swarmed by Somalis. It drove home to me how quickly the Somalis can come out of nowhere and close in on you.

A few days after his arrival in the country, Mike found himself on the roof of the "White House." The White House compound sheltered the FAST Company Platoon, which provided security for the embassy, and their command operations center. The State Department personnel stayed there, and all of the armored Suburbans and the armored HMMWVs (high-mobility multipurpose wheeled vehicles) they used for their armed convoy escorts were kept there. It was the old living quarters of the U.S. ambassador. The ambassador and his staff had moved into trailers in the same compound. They had large, ten-foot-high walls built in front of the trailers for their protection.

It was midafternoon in June, and Mike and Sergeant M, the senior sniper from the platoon he was relieving, were on the rooftop of the White House compound going over the range card. "It was the rooftop post manned by a FAST Marine but wasn't the dedicated sniper post until later in my deployment." (A range card is a hand-drawn document that graphically represents the range distance to specific locations that is easily recognized by the shooter and observer and terrain in front of you. It lays out the assigned target reference points with the corresponding distance and azimuth to that location as well as the data you need to dial on the scope to hit a target at that location.) While baking in the Somali sun and inhaling the scent of burning trash, Mike glanced around the area that stretched out in front of him and noticed two tribal clans fighting on the dusty streets below outside the compound. "They usually started midmorning and continued through most of the day." He diverted his attention off the range card and down to the streets below. He could see there were about twenty to thirty clansmen, and they were armed with AK-47s, PRK machine guns, 12.7 and 14.5 machine guns, and rocket-propelled grenades (RPGs). Within minutes, the tribal clansmen started shooting at each other. They were approximately three hundred to four hundred yards away from where Mike was standing. It was a full-on firefight. Minutes later, Mike heard the crack of a bullet piercing the hot air as it passed overhead. "I looked at Sergeant M, he looked at me, and I asked him, 'Are they shooting at us?' Sergeant M just looked at me and shrugged his shoulders. We didn't know if they were shooting as us or if it was just spillover fire from the firefight below. So . . . we continued to go over the range car. We didn't call it in, because with just the one shot it could have been just a stray bullet or a ricochet. But then another round cracked closer this time. We looked at each other and shook our heads, saying, 'Yep, they're getting closer.' After another round passed even closer, we thought, "Oh shit! They are getting a bead on us!"

Sergeant M looked through the scope of his M40, and Mike glassed the area with binoculars. They were as low as they could possibly get while still trying to observe the surrounding area and the clansmen, and then another bullet came whizzing by, but this one passed right between them. "I dove right and he dove left! Once I checked on Sergeant M, the other sniper, to make sure he was ok, I turned the crank of the TA-312 [field phone] and radioed to the COC (Combat Operations Center) saying that we were taking fire. Their reply was, 'It's just spillover fire.' My reply was they were full of shit! Sergeant M agreed with me. We never could identify the shooter. I had loud ringing and was deaf in my left ear the rest of the day; Sergeant M was deaf in his right ear. I have issues still today with my ear from that shot. We observed the area but couldn't ID the shooter. We didn't take any more fire that day."

The FAST Platoon Mike was in was broken down into two sections; Sergeant T led one and Mike led the other. The platoon had two school-trained snipers, Corporal R and Mike; three Designated Marksmen (DMs); two lance corporals, L and P, and Corporal M (he was a DM and also a graduate of Amphibious Reconnaissance School [ARS]); and Corporal B, another ARS graduate. They all assumed and carried out the duties of their "normal" jobs: squad leader, fire team leader, and so on.

In Mogadishu we only did snipering when a situation arose. Conducting reconnaissance and surveillance is not as exciting and sexy as conducting the assault or being in the assault element. We didn't do this type of work at FAST; I did it when I was at 3/6 [Battalion Landing Team 3/6 Scout Sniper Platoon]. Usually we would insert two or three days before the assault to conduct preassault reconnaissance and close-in surveillance. We would observe the target building to confirm or deny information (for example, was the target individual or the device really there?). We would try to recognize any patterns, such as the location of guards and where they patrolled, we would try to identify areas that were commonly used and those that weren't, and we tried to identify any entrances and access points to the buildings, etc. But a lot of it was lying motionless hour after hour with nothing going on and having to be as still and as quiet as humanly possible. You start to hear your breathing, and it seems to get louder the quieter you are, and you think to yourself, can they hear it? We wait there until we link up with the assault force so we can guide them to the target, and cover them by precision rifle fire if needed. In essence, the assault force has what some would call the cool job of raiding the building, but they need our info and precision rifle fire to cover them.

Just a few days later another incident happened.

A few weeks after my platoon arrived we had a few days to turn over with 1st Platoon FAST; then they departed, and we, 2nd Platoon FAST, took over. I was on the roof again doing some sketches of the area to document the terrain in front of our position to ensure nothing changed over the time we were there. Dead Cow Road, named from the previous platoon, and you can guess why, paralleled the compound wall in front of me. Market Street was slightly off to my right and went perpendicular away from the compound and into the Medina Hospital area. Further off to my left about five hundred to six hundred yards ran Afgoye Road, which paralleled Market Street. Dead Cow Road dead-ended into Afgoye Road. I assigned different teams to sketch the area in front of the compound and the abandoned building at the intersection of Dead Cow Road and Market Street. I wanted to make sure no one added to the debris or knocked out any shooting ports close to one of our posts. A shooting port is the window we shoot through. While I was sketching the area, I observed a few technical vehicles pull up on Afgoye road and stop. A technical vehicle, or "technical," was usually a pickup truck with a mounted crew-served weapon on the back. We had compiled a list of technicals we had observed over time. We would report them in detail when we saw them, but after the third time we put them on the list. We found that some of the clans would change weapons on the same vehicle to make it appear they had more technicals than they really had. The area between Afgoye Road and Market Street was pretty much open terrain except for some piles of trash, rocks, and rubble here and there. The right side of Market Street had a stone wall that stood about four or five feet tall. A large number of clansmen got off the back of a technical and some cling-on trucks on Afgoye Road. (We called large dump trucks or box-type trucks that would transport large numbers of people who would literally cling on or hold on to the vehicle "cling-on" trucks.) They started to spread out and in groups of two to four behind large rock piles that were spread haphazardly across the open area in front of me. They began bounding (bounding is when one group would move from one covered position to the next while the others cover their movement by either observation or fire) one group at a time as they worked their way down to Market Street. I looked over at the Marine on Post 2 (also on the roof of the White House) to make sure he was observing what I was . . . and he was. I continued to sketch while keeping an eye on their progression.

Once they reached the stone wall on Market Street, they began to spread out fairly evenly as if manning a defensive position. Then I noticed one clansman move from position to position, talking and pointing to each individual as if assigning sectors of fire. They weren't aiming at the compound or me; they had moved left to right in front of me and were to my right now. After this guy went to each individual he called them all into a huddle. They talked for a few minutes then broke up, got on the technical and the cling-on truck, and drove off. I was left with a very disconcerting feeling in my gut. I asked the post stander if he was going to call that in to the COC. He said, "What do you mean? They didn't shoot anything." I was like, "They just did a rehearsal! They got online, bounded by teams all the way to the wall where the leader assigned sectors of fire. And then they conducted a debrief!" His reply was, "Oh." I couldn't believe it. We just watched this event go down together at the same exact time, and he couldn't put two and two together. We [snipers] aren't trained just to shoot or to shoot when we are being shot at; we are trained to assess, to analyze, and to observe. Throughout my training and the years of service I had in up to that point I was able to put it all together. After I finished the sketch I was working on I told the COC, as well as Sergeant K, our intel [intelligence] Marine assigned to the platoon from the Marine Corps Security Force Battalion about what I observed.

It wasn't long before another, similar incident happened.

On another afternoon, a few weeks later in July, the COG was out taking pictures of different technicals driving by and happened to capture a picture of a dump truck carrying a quad-mounted gun from a ZSU-23-4. (We referred to three smaller rotating groups of post standers and their supervisor as the Corporals of the Guard. The "COG" specifically refers to the leader/supervisor, which was normally a corporal.) One of the regular (infantry) Marines (we called them "post standers") on Post 2 didn't see it. The COG turned over the camera roll to Sergeant K. He turned it over to a co-located agency to develop. The pictures confirmed what the COG reported. At that point I felt like we needed to have the snipers and DMs consolidate and stand Post 2, not just infantry Marines. This was the second time an infantry Marine on Post 2 missed a significant event. No fault to the Marine; he wasn't trained in observation skills at our level of analysis, plus it was too large an area to observe for one Marine. I brought it to Captain B's attention, and he agreed that Post 2 needed to have the trained observers such as snipers, DMs, and amphibious reconnaissance school graduates to stand that post. Post 2 was the critical post because from Post 2 you had a 360-degree observation of the whole compound. We could see and cover all the other posts on the compound.

In August, Mike took over the R&S section. "We broke up into three, two-man teams: Corporal M and I, Corporals R and B, and Lance Corporals L and P (who just happened to be partners at DM School). From that time until we got the word we would be pulling the USLO out of Mogadishu, we stood six-hour watches—six on, twelve off—for over a month. Once we started standing post on the roof, we worked with Sergeant K to help figure out the atmospherics and track the clans throughout the city. He used our reports to help fill out a twenty-four-hour pattern analysis sheet. Anytime there was a gunshot in the city, we would log the time, direction, estimated distance (from Post 2), and the number of rounds fired in a notebook. This helped him, along with other assets, to track Aidid's clan throughout Mogadishu." See, they aren't just shooters.

Some background information on General Mohamed Farrah Hassan Aidid: he was a former intelligence officer under Somalia President Mohamed Siad Barre's regime. Barre suspected Aidid of planning a coup d'etat and imprisoned him for six years. Aidid's clan managed to overthrow Barre. With no successor to Barre's regime, civil war broke out, and "warlords," a term born in Somalia during this time, were claiming to be the de facto rulers of the country. Aidid was one of these "warlords." On October 3, 1993, President Clinton sent in elite U.S forces to capture Aidid and his militia in Mogadishu. Many of you remember what ensued, which was captured in the movie *Black Hawk Down*. (Mike was off the coast of Haiti in October 1993 when this event happened, but he watched it as his in-brief when he arrived in Somalia.) The United States withdrew its forces soon afterward, and the United Nations left Somalia in 1995, after which Aidid declared himself president of Somalia in June 1995. On July 24, 1996, Aidid and his militia were in battle with the forces of warlords and former Aidid allies. Aidid was wounded by gunfire during the fight and ultimately suffered a fatal heart attack on August 1, 1996.

(As a side note, after Mike left Somalia, while in 3/6 Scout Sniper Platoon with then Staff Sergeant K, the S-2 Chief [S-2 stands for the intelligence section of the Marine Corps], he used this same pattern analysis technique again in Egypt to help track firing and other incidents in the area of operations. While he was on patrol with his sniper team, when they heard gunfire, they would halt, take a knee, and the assistant team leader would get out the GPS and get a grid while Mike shot an azimuth and estimated the range. He would call all that information back to the battalion. Once he did, they picked up and started moving again. They repeated these steps every time they heard gunfire. The other team leader started to pick up on the calls and quickly started doing the same. Now the battalion was able to triangulate where the fire was coming from.)

Around early September we got the word the USLO was going to be pulling out of Mogadishu, so our platoon restructured for this move. All the embassy gear had to be moved to the airport in preparation for a flight to Kenya. One section was guarding the gear at the airport, another section was escorting the convoy, and myself and a group of about eight to ten Marines were holding down the embassy compound. As the platoon was getting ready to depart on a convoy, one of the posts reported that a checkpoint was being manned by local clansmen on Afgoye Road just inside our area of observation, about six hundred to seven hundred yards away from Post 2 in the compound. As the SOG (sergeant of the guard), I went to the roof of the White House to Post 2 to survey the situation myself. I called the platoon commander to inform him there was indeed a checkpoint set up by the locals, and it was being manned by a few clansmen and a technical that had a 106 recoilless rifle on it. The clansmen were stopping vehicles and people to extort money to pass—yes, you can do that in Somalia. The platoon commander told me to take it out (the makeshift checkpoint) if they aimed their 106 recoilless rifle toward the compound, because it was capable of punching holes in our perimeter walls and the walls to the White House, which was where our embassy was located. I said, "Roger that." As the convoy departed, my sniper partner Corporal M and I manned the roof; me with my M40 and Corporal M with his DMR and the M49 spotting scope in between us. We set up and with the appropriate range dialed on the scopes. After about an hour or so I decided to check the rest of the post, since I was the SOG and we only had a handful of Marines left to guard it. It was quiet, and the technical wasn't aiming at the compound. About twenty minutes went by, and I get contacted by Corporal M on the radio saying the checkpoint had left. "Good," I thought to myself. I told him to put my rifle in its case but to leave it up there, and we both returned to the COC, which was on the first floor of the White House. Thirty minutes later I got a call that the checkpoint was back up, and now the 106 was manned and pointing at the compound! M and I jumped into action. We both put our gear on, our helmets and our ranger vests, and raced back up to the roof. Our ranger vests were green camo vests that had a small arms protective insert (SAPI) which was a thick ballistic plate sewn in the front to stop bullets. In 1994 that was not the normal gear that Marines had or used, because that technology hadn't made it to the regular infantry units and was generally only for special operations forces, but we were issued them over there. As soon as I got to the post, I looked through the M49 spotting scope we had left set up. Sure enough, the 106 was manned and pointing directly at us. I bent down to get my rifle out of the case and set it up on the sandbag. I quickly double-checked the range card and the data on the gun, racked the bolt, and sighted in. In those short few seconds that it took me to do all of that, the Somali local who was manning the 106 spun the rifle away from the compound and jumped down off the technical.

Mike didn't know what to do; should he take the shot, because when he first got to the roof his rules of engagement (ROE) were met? There was a weapon and potential violence of action. In his mind, the fact that the 106 was just aiming at the compound was violence of action. One shot from that would have breached the wall enough for the enemy to make entry. On the other hand, he was thinking about what he saw when he was actually behind the rifle, which didn't meet the ROE. In the back of his mind he thought if things got bad and it turned into a shit storm, there were only seven other Marines on the compound to defend it; but he had no doubt that they could defend it competently with the pre-positioned posts they had set up. His concern was the bigger picture: what happens if the returning convoy gets stuck out in town because there was an attack on the embassy, or the USLO can't pull out because of an uprising in Mogadishu—what if it turns into another Black Hawk Down incident? Again the thought of the long-range implications, not just about taking a shot, but all of the follow-on consequences. "I made the decision in a split second; I didn't take the shot. As part of the years of training I have gone through, I learned how to take the shot, when to take the shot, and sometimes more importantly, when not to take the shot. You have to look at the bigger picture and think about the unit's mission, not just my team's mission. I feel I made the correct call that day. I don't think the Somalis realized they were aiming at the compound but quickly realized it as we were running up the outside steps to post two on the roof; hence why they scrambled to move the rifle and jump off the vehicle."

The U.S. pulled the U.S. flag down on September 15, 1994, when the last of the diplomatic personnel and the Marines from FAST Company 2nd Platoon departed the American compound in Mogadishu. The diplomatic personnel went to Nairobi, Kenya, and the Marines went to Mombasa, Kenya, then back to the United States. Mike's Somalia deployment gave him real-world experience and the confidence that would help him throughout the rest of his career. "I enjoyed this mission so much that I remember as my platoon time was winding down getting ready to head back home, Sergeant K and I were going to ask to stay and transfer to the platoon replacing ours just so we could stay, because of the tremendous responsibility we had as sergeants. I'll never forget the steak and lobster grilled up on Sundays! That was some of the best lobster I have ever had!

2004/KABUL, AFGHANISTAN (OPERATION ENDURING FREEDOM): USING A LESSON LEARNED

It was fall of 2004 when the Marine Corps had redesignated the 4th Marine Expeditionary Brigade (MEB) to be an Antiterrorism Brigade. The infantry battalion that fell under 4th MEB(AT) was being sent overseas to guard high-risk posts providing external embassy security. "The Marine Security Guard (MSG) was the internal security; think dress-blue-clad Marines as interior guards at the embassies. We were tasked with external security. I was assigned to 'F' Company 2/6; the battalion that fell under the 4th MEB(AT). My battalion was assigned to send Marines to the embassies in Iraq and Afghanistan to provide security. One company was assigned to be the quick reaction force (QRF) in Afghanistan for Afghanistan's President, Hamid Karzai, during the elections. One company was assigned embassy security in Kabul and one company in Baghdad, Iraq. My company (F Co) was sent to Kabul."

While serving as a rifle company gunnery sergeant in Kabul, Afghanistan, as part of the 4th MEB(AT), Mike was stationed at the U.S. embassy compound in Kabul with his rifle company (minus approximately ninety Marines). (As an author side note, the afterword to this book is a story about the incident that happened at this embassy on May 22, 2003, where a Marine sniper shot an Afghan National Army soldier in the head when he aimed a rifle directly at the Marines on post at the embassy.) Shortly after his company relieved the previous company there, while on post, one of the DMs spotted two men outside the compound with a cell phone and binoculars. They reported the suspicious behavior to the advanced targeting intelligence cell (ATIC) section—the collective group of Marines comprising intelligence Marines from our battalion and counterintelligence Marines. The Marines from the ATIC cell quickly got their gear on and set out to find these individuals. The DMs didn't have any reference points close to the location of these two individuals, and because of this, they had a difficult time trying to guide the ATIC Marines to the exact location. The area was large and open and had few identifying terrain features or man-made structures to help narrow down the location. Mike was up on the roof with the DMs while they were trying to guide the ATIC Marines to the targets.

> I was kind of kicking myself in the ass for not seeing this problem sooner. I went down to the ATIC section and got one of the intel Marines to print me off overhead imagery of the embassy and the surrounding area. I got a ruler, made some tick marks, gridded out the whole thing, and put letters across the top and numbers down the left side. We taught and used GRGs [gridded reference graphics] in my last unit, Special Operations Training Group, and at 3/6 Scout Sniper Platoon, very successfully, so why not use it now! Unfortunately, it was too late to help that night, and we lost the two targets. I made copies of the GRG I created and passed them to all the posts to use in the future to help identify exact target locations in situations when you have nothing else to go by. I flew back to the States a week later and was told by the Company 1st Sergeant that the

ambassador liked it so much, they did it on a larger scale and covered the whole city in this method.

There may not be anything sexy about gridding out area, lying motionless in a position for hours observing, or standing by on a ship running mission rehearsals, but that is part of being a sniper, an efficacious sniper, and you have to love all parts of the job if you want to be a U.S. Marine Chief Scout Sniper.

AFTER THE COMBAT

In October 2009 I was transferred from the Gunner at 2/2 to the Infantry Training Battalion, School of Infantry at Camp Geiger in North Carolina. 2/2 had just deployed to Afghanistan. Once 2/2 started taking casualties, I started going to visit them at the hospital in Bethesda (Maryland) so they could see a familiar face. On one such trip to Bethesda in late November or early December, I was walking through the halls on my way to one of the Marines' rooms when I heard a voice. As soon as I heard it, I said in my mind, that's "the freak show." I backed up and saw the name on board outside the room: "SSgt R." I could hear him talking, so I knocked on the door and went in. He was lying in the bed with his foot in traction. He had survived an IED [improvised explosive device] strike to his Oshkosh MRAP, and his foot took some serious damage. In the room with him were his wife and father. A minute or so after I entered the doorway to the room, he kicked his wife out. I felt very uncomfortable and wasn't sure what was going on. Once she was gone, he turned to his father and said, "Gunner Carr was my first squad leader. When I reenlist, and every day, I try to be half the Marine and man he trained me to be. And that I do what I do because of how he trained me and the leadership he showed me while we were at FAST." That blew me away. I only ever did what I was trained to do, and that was to take care of my Marines and train them to the best of my ability. I tried to teach my squad at FAST something every morning, simple classes like the elements of call for fire, how to cross danger areas, reporting, how to make field expedient antennas, etc. I didn't realize I had such an impact on their lives. I was truly humbled.

Being sent to FAST and then deploying to Somalia and Iraq, then to Afghanistan ultimately landed Mike in a successful place today. And now he is a retired CWO4 Marine Gunner.

I met the best group of Marines I have had the pleasure of serving with. I have just about done everything I want to. My only regret is the toll it took on my marriage and ultimately my family. Before I would go on my combat deployments, I would start compartmentalizing feelings and prepare myself for what I had to do and what I might see. In doing so, I inadvertently was distancing myself from my wife, who needed me to be there for her emotionally because she was battling her own struggles worrying about my safety, having the full responsibility of taking care of our children, and everyday life situations. I cut off my emotions to prepare for the emotional stress I knew I was going to have to endure, and she took it as cutting off my emotions to her. If I could go back in time, would I have done things differently? Yes, one thing. I see the toll it has taken on my kids, sharing time between their mother and I. If I could go back in time, I would have tried to express my emotions better so she could understand what I was going through. I wished I could have communicated better. We are divorced now, and my kids have grown up with my deployments and the divorce. They have taken the greatest toll. It breaks my heart to see the pain I have caused them. My son Michael and my daughter Laura are two special and amazing people. And when I see how they have really come into their own, I feel so proud. They give me my most pride and joy. I'm retired now, and I have given what I can to this country; now it is time to focus on them.

2

TOO YOUNG FOR COMBAT

WAS IT FROM "WAR IN THE WOODS"?

Dave's parents used to tell him he played "war in the woods" when he was a child for as long as they could remember. "War in the woods" was a game he and his friends made up in which they would run around the woods slinging paintballs, and whatever else they could find to use as ammunition, at each other while trying to capture the flag of the "enemy." Maybe this childhood game was the origin of his fascination and fixation with the military, which soon led him down the unforeseen path to a promising military career later in life. He remembers his father telling him as a kid, "You'll never make any money playing with guns."

Dave and his family grew up in northern Virginia. If you have ever lived there or been there, you know it is very common to see military personnel working in the area, and it is not uncommon to see a convoy of military vehicles rolling down I-95 from time to time. Dave's father worked for a government consulting firm, wearing a suit to work every day, inside the Beltway, an idiom for the area that encompasses the Washington, D.C., metropolitan area; parts of northern Virginia; and some parts of Maryland. Although heavily involved in the government, his dad never donned a military uniform. Dave couldn't identify any one event or circumstance as the catalyst that got him interested in the military, war, and guns at such an early age. But as far back as he could remember, all he ever wanted to do was grow up and be in the military. Both of his grandfathers were drafted during World War II, and his great-grandfather served in World War I. Even so, it wasn't like they sat around the fireplace sharing their war stories with Dave. His was the typical suburban family; they weren't the adventurous, outdoorsy types. They didn't go on camping trips, he and his father didn't hunt, and no one in his family owned a firearm. Looking back now, Dave laughs because of the irony of what his father used to say to him as a child; *playing with guns* is exactly how Dave makes his money, and he's made a decent career out of it as well. At the age of nineteen, Dave was not only a United States Marine Corps (USMC) Scout Sniper, he also became a weapons expert and the go-to guy when it came to identifying foreign weapons and ammunition while he was deployed in Iraq. His intense enthusiasm for the sport of shooting led him to start his own business after the Marine Corps, called D&D GunWorks and Refinishing, LLC. The business specializes in gunsmithing, and his partner is a former USMC match grade armorer.

When Dave was about ten years old, his friend's father let him shoot a gun. Dave can't recall what type of gun it was, but he'll never forget the rush he felt from firing it. Shooting that gun gave him such a thrill, it had an everlasting impression on him. Having just seen a sniper movie with Tom Berenger, and having read books about Carlos Hathcock, Dave became obsessed with Marine Scout Snipers, and at the age of ten he decided he was going to be one. Carlos Hathcock is one of the most famous USMC Scout Snipers and is legendary among the Marine Corps. He is known for having ninety-three confirmed kills during his career: ninety-three. His nickname was "White Feather," given by the Vietcong and the North Vietnamese Army because of the white feather he used to keep in the band of his bush hat. But what most people may not know is that another USMC Scout Sniper surpassed his kills. "Actually, Chuck Mawhinney has the most confirmed kills recorded: 103. He is a close personal friend now."

When eighth grade came around, Dave remembers he had to complete a school project (he believes it was called "out to work day" or something like that) where the students would shadow someone in a career field that they wanted to be in when they grew up. Then they would have to write about it afterward. He had read somewhere that the Marine Corps had a Scout Sniper School located in Quantico, Virginia, which was only about thirty minutes from where he lived. With no hesitation, or permission, he picked up the phone and called their public relations number, which he found in the phone book, to see if he could go visit (his exact words were "hang out") with the Schoolhouse for a day. He was certain he would be rejected because he was just a kid who wanted to "hang out" with highly trained Marine Corps Snipers; his backup plan was to go with his friend to his father's office for a brutally boring day. To his surprise, however, the Marine Corps granted his wish and gave him permission to visit the Scout Sniper School and Marine Corps base in Quantico for the day.

"There I was, a thirteen-year-old kid sitting in the classroom where the best-trained snipers in the world went. I asked question after question on everything and anything I could think of, not only about what was being taught. I asked about different types of weapons and their capabilities, and how it hard was to be a Marine and get into that school." The instructors welcomed him and admired his fervor. He knew he was mentally prepping himself to be sitting in that very same classroom one day, but as a Marine student. When he left the school that day, he made a pact with himself; he decided he would do whatever it took to earn the title of Marine Corps Scout Sniper. Little did he know when he made his declaration that day, in a few short years the longest war in U.S. history would start, and in two years after that he would be sitting in that classroom, not as a grade-schooler for a report, but as a Marine to be taught the skills he needed for the biggest test of his life: facing combat as a Marine Scout Sniper at the age of nineteen.

People who are able to live out their dreams, whether for a moment or as a career, are lucky, to say the least. I was one of those people just like Dave. Ever since watching a TV special on King Tut's tomb with pharaohs and pyramids as a twelve-year-old, and then watching Indiana Jones movies as a teenager, I was determined to be an archaeologist. No one told me (except for my father, who, much like Dave's father, told me, "You'll never make money digging up rocks!") that it would be extremely hard to find a job as an archaeologist. Perhaps he was right, because after graduation I found myself with a master's degree from Brown University in old world archaeology and art, with no job and no money. Perhaps I didn't try hard enough? Perhaps I wasn't smart enough? Whatever the reason, six months after graduation and return-ing from a dig on an Etruscan temple in beautiful Tuscany, on a whim, I joined the Navy Reserves. People are always amazed when they hear my background: first an archaeologist, then a Military Interrogator. Most can't make the connection. There really is none; it was just life circumstances and opportunities. Just like Dave, though, no one in my family had been in the military—well, at least willingly—nor had they made a career out of it. My father was drafted during World War II in the Army, and when I told him I was going to join the Navy Reserves, he scrunched up his nose and said, "What! Are you crazy?" He was not too happy with my decision. He was an MP (Military Police), and he would tell me horrific stories of having to lift body bags off air flights that contained the bodies of deceased soldiers. He said that the contents of some of those bags sloshed around as he lifted them off the trucks. I can't even imagine having to do that. So I can understand his harsh hesitation and resistance to my joining the military, because his memo-ries are not that pleasant. Nevertheless, on November 14, 1997, I was raising my right hand and getting sworn in to my duty of six mandatory years of service with the Navy Reserves as an Intelligence Specialist. That decision, my whim, was one of the best decisions I've made, and I can tell you that Dave's decision to enlist in the USMC and to follow his passion was one of his best, or *the* best, too.

Shortly after returning from his visit to Quantico, still attending middle school, he decided he would be enlisting in the Marines; he knew this would come as a surprise to his parents, who had always just assumed he would go to college. He knew that he had to enlist in the Marine Corps if he wanted to attend the Scout Sniper School, because officers are generally not permitted to attend. Dave was a sophomore in high school when the events of 9/11 happened. "Before the terror attack, I was sitting in world history class; [the teacher] was a Vietnam vet who flew spotter planes to mark positions for fast movers. He turned on the TV after hearing the first tower was hit, and we all watched the second tower get hit. Then we started to hear word that the Pentagon got hit. Shortly after that, a lot of kids were getting pulled out of school. Many of our parents worked in the Pentagon, and we didn't know who was alive or dead. There were a bunch of kids wondering what was going on. The movie *Red Dawn* quickly came to mind." If he ever had any second thoughts of possibly going along with what his parents expected him to do, they ceased that day. Serving and protecting his country, which was now at war, was his only priority. Dave knew he didn't want to miss out on fighting for his country during "his generation's war." As he shared his story with me that day, he told me, "I had no idea we would still be at war while I am writing this."

The day after he turned seventeen he enlisted in the USMC delayed entry program, before his senior year of high school. His parents had to sign a waiver to allow him to join and were still not pleased that he was choosing the Marines over college. With conviction, he met with a Marine Corps recruiter to enlist. What happened next threw him for a loop. You would think recruiters would jump for joy when someone walks into their office and says, "Sign me up!" After all, they have certain quotas to meet for getting new recruits to sign up for service, and if they don't meet them, they won't be getting a good fitness report. When someone walks in off the street willingly to sign a binding military contract for a certain number of years, that's an easy sell.

I was recruited in the most common sense of the word. I had a friend who had just joined the Navy Reserve as an Intelligence Specialist, and he pitched the program to me. At first I told him he was crazy and ridiculous to even suggest it to me. But then I thought, what the hell, it's a challenge, it will be fun, and I needed the money. A month later I was raising my hand, getting sworn into the U.S. Navy Reserves as an "E3." (E3 is an acronym for the third enlisted rank in the U.S. Navy.) When I arrived to my very first official training weekend, everyone, said, "Your recruiter screwed you." The recruiter knew what he was doing; he needed to meet quotas. He wasn't about to suggest I try to come in as a commissioned officer. Apparently if you have a master's degree you can come into the Reserves as an officer rank in some cases. I've seen lawyers and doctors come in as lieutenant commanders (the fourth officer rank in the Navy). No matter; the recruiter did me a favor that day. I enjoyed my time as an enlisted member and am very thankful I was one. I didn't speak military, so I needed to learn from the ground up.

However, Dave's recruiters actually tried to convince him to NOT join the Marines and instead seriously look at attending college! They told him that they wanted him to take the SAT as well. Who would turn away an applicant ready to sign on the dotted line? Apparently Dave's ASVAB (Armed Services Vocational Aptitude Battery test, which helps predict in what occupational area you'll be successful in the military) scores were high, coupled with the fact he was being looked at by a number of colleges for track scholarships. This made a him a good candidate for college acceptance. At least his recruiters were honest with him. But he explained to them that all he wanted to be was a USMC Scout Sniper. The recruiters explained to Dave what it took to become a Scout Sniper and that "the odds" were not on his side. They told him even if he had the skill and ability, luck plays a huge part in just getting a shot at trying out (you have to be asked to apply and get accepted). Then you have to somehow get to a battalion holding an indoc (short and a common slang word for *indoctrination*), be granted permission to take the indoc, pass the indoc, then be recommended to go to Scout Sniper School. It's a very select group of people who become Scout Snipers. Being determined, on the verge of stubborn, he didn't care. He was going for it.

In June 2004, at the age of seventeen, Dave graduated from high school, and a few weeks later found himself on Parris Island, not to be confused with the romanticized European city. He was in boot camp in South Carolina at the Marine Corps Recruit Depot Parris Island being issued an M16A2. He spent countless days getting yelled at to run or make a bed or memorize orders, all of which he followed respectfully and promptly up until his graduation with a meritorious promotion; "It was a little extra money, and that was nice." Boot camp was not hard for Dave; it was the stepping-stone to bigger and better things. Infantry school was next; now the training gets real. He was able to select "assaultman" as his MOS (Military Occupational Specialty). He graduated at the top of his class and was meritoriously promoted for it. He thought to himself, "I'm doing it."

Dave arrived at the unit he was assigned to, Fox Company, Camp Lejeune, North Carolina, 2nd Battalion/6th Marines (2/6), in early January of 2005. When he checked in, most of the company had already been deployed to Afghanistan, so he was sent to an M2 Heavy Machine-gunners course and passed successfully. It was after that training he was told about the STA (Surveillance and Target Acquisition; pronounced *stay*) Platoon; this was the Scout Snipers platoon within an infantry battalion. He was getting closer and closer to his mark. When he inquired about the process to be selected for the STA Platoon, he was told that selection board would be held soon. The only problem was, his staff sergeant didn't want to lose Dave as an "0351" (Assaultman, Anti-armor and Demolitions). When the week of the selection board came, that particular staff sergeant just happened to be attending another course. The corporal who was left in charge was not a big fan of the staff sergeant, so he encouraged Dave to just go to the selection board. Not sure of who signed off on what or who didn't like whom, Dave adhered to the corporal's suggestion and went without hesitation. Dave ended up able to attend the board for Scout Sniper selection.

The first part of what became a living hell for the weeks to come started off innocent enough in the "Service Record Book" screening. This is where the leaders of the STA Platoon look at your service record and decide, first, if you have the minimum requirements to even be part of this selection board; second, if you are in exceptional physical condition (which is documented annually in your service record); and third, if you had already qualified as an expert rifleman. Once it's determined you have met the prequalifying criteria, you are now allowed to sit before "the board."

The lights were out in the back of the room, and we entered the room one at a time. The lighting was set up purposefully so you couldn't see anyone's face and you wouldn't know who was asking you questions, nor would you know their rank or age. I remember being nervous, and being asked all sorts of questions, from "Why should you be here?" to questions about specific types of weapons capabilities. The one question I remember most vividly was "What is transonic range?" I had learned a lot up to that point, both self-taught and from my formal Marine Corps training schools, but I had no idea what this was. I racked my brain trying to think of what the hell it could be. I drew a blank. The silence as they waited for my answer was deafening. It was soon broken, however, by one of the faceless voices berating me for not knowing. I was told to step outside and wait. There were maybe twenty of us that day, I can't remember, going before the board, all with high hopes of being accepted to the elite Scout Sniper training. (By the way, transonic range is the range at which a projectile is no longer flying above the speed of sound; it generally becomes unstable at this point and begins to degrade in accuracy greatly. I have never forgotten that definition, along with a few others, to this day.) As I stood against a wall waiting outside that dark room, feeling defeated, all I could think was that they were going to call me back in only to tell me to go back to my company. After a couple of hours had passed, one of the Scout Snipers from the platoon came out and pulled people in the room again one by one. We were all told to go back to our companies, and that was it. "Was it over?" I thought to myself. I assumed I didn't make the cut. I left defeated. I have never wanted something so badly.

The next morning Dave woke up about 0530 to someone knocking on his door. "It was a sergeant from the STA Platoon. He said that I needed to go to chow (breakfast) and then come back to pack some things that I thought I needed for the field for a week, because I was going out with them for an assessment. I was thrilled and did as he said; went to chow and went back to pack my gear. I had never packed my gear before without a packing list; up until that point I had always been given a list of what I needed to pack. Now, I had to pack independent of any list or orders; this was a new thing for me. I went off my gear list I used from my last field exercise, which seemed like a good idea. Shortly after I finished packing, the sergeant came to get me. He told me to put my gear in the HMMWV that was waiting downstairs. He also said in a low soft voice, 'From now on, you run everywhere you go.' His stoic face turned into an evil smile." And run Dave did.

FIRST DEPLOYMENT: FALLUJAH, SEPTEMBER 2005

Dave deployed to Fallujah in 2005, some nine months after Phantom Fury; he relieved 1st Battalion/6th Marines (1/6). There was a period of calm between Phantom Fury and when 1/6 departed, but the fighting picked up again around the fall of '05. "IEDs (improvised explosive devices) were big then." Dave landed in Kuwait like everyone else who is on their way to the "sandbox." From there, he hopped on C130 to TQ (Dave can't remember the name; everyone just called it "TQ"). That was the first time he had been on a C130. He doesn't know how many of them were in the plane, but he says they were all packed in there like sardines. The pilots had to do evasive maneuvers as they landed because of the threat of commonly occurring RPG (rocket-propelled grenade launcher) attacks. Dave remembers one of the guys in his platoon, who had been on this flight before, looked over at Dave, who was holding a .50-caliber SASR (special-application scoped rifle, pronounced *sass-ser*), which weighed about thirty pounds, and over the roar of the engines he yelled to Dave, "Let go of the SASR!" Dave didn't think he heard him clearly. Confused, he kept a grip on it. As Dave watched, this guy removed his hands from his gun and signaled to Dave to do the same. Still confused, Dave complied and let go of his SASR. They were in their approach, spiraling down through the air like mating eagles, and all of a sudden the SASR became weightless and hovered a few inches above the deck. He thought that was pretty cool; it took his mind off of possibly being shot at by the enemy, at least. Dave was nineteen at this point, the youngest guy in the platoon. He didn't have a clue as to what was going on, yet he seemed to be quite at home amid the chaos, excitement, and fear. As the SASR hovered, and not knowing if he should be more excited or scared, he began to reflect on how he got into that seat on that plane that day. He was living his dream, or soon would be. The plane landed safely, and everyone went immediately to a tent for the indoc brief (the safety brief for this country). The tent wasn't a typical army-green military tent you'd picture in your head; it was a Bedouin tent with tassels hanging everywhere. The indoc brief covered what to do if they came under enemy attack, what bunkers to take shelter in, and so on. Then they were told to grab some rounds (ammunition) and chow, then get settled in and prepare to move in the morning. Dave went to his assigned living quarters (another tent) and was lying on his cot with a bunch of other guys. All of a sudden the air raid sirens blasted off; this was about twenty minutes after the indoc brief. He had no clue what was going on; he assumed they were going to take incoming fire. He jumped off his cot, grabbed his flak, and looked around to notice none of the other guys were moving. One of the sergeants was just lying there calmly on his cot, listening to his headphones. He rolled over and said to Dave, "Don't worry about it. Number one, we're in a tent. If you get up and run, one of those rounds will find you. And two, if a round comes in here, that flak is not going to do you any good. So just lay down, get some rest, and relax." Dave thought to himself, "Well, okay then. I guess I can do that." They never heard any impact, so they

weren't sure why the air raid sirens went off. Apparently it was commonplace that the sirens went off half the time for no reason. I asked
Dave if that sound put the fear in him, as I would imagine it would me,
and he said, "It wasn't overly scary; it became as common of a sound as
the local fire department whistles back home."

His first night in Iraq had come and gone with no incidents. Now was
his first official day "in country." Dave mounted a truck that would take
him to his camp, Camp Baharia, right outside of Fallujah. "It seemed
to take forever to get there. It's a pretty well-known camp; it was like a
resort where all the nefarious activities went on with Saddam's sons. We
were taken to our hooches (their living quarters) and then got another
indoc brief." They were told they were in an active combat zone and
to make sure they had their weapons with them at all times and ammo
close by, because they might take direct fire. They were supposed to get
two hot meals a day at the chow hall there, but for some reason Dave
doesn't ever recall having two hot meals a day while he was in Iraq.
The food wasn't cooked there; it was brought in from elsewhere. It was
like a giant tub of slop, but it was hot. He lived mostly on MREs (meal
ready-to-eat packages) or whatever they could find in town, which he
preferred over the MREs or the slop.

Dave's team's first mission was to Saqlawiyah (they called it Saq), a
town west of Fallujah. It was a pretty, green, and lush area with lots of
palm trees. Dave and his team went over the plan of where they were
getting inserted and what they had to look for. No kill targets or anything
cool like that. They were just assessing the lay of the land and getting
their feet wet; this was his very first mission in combat. (His team leader
had already been in combat before.) There were four of them setting
out for a three-day mission. (Reminds me of *Gilligan's Island* when the
crew set out for a three-hour tour and disaster followed.) Approximately
twenty minutes after they got inserted into the town, weighted down
with all their gear, they started taking several rounds of small-arms fire.
The rounds were hitting close by, so they were sure they were targets,
but nothing impacted them, and then the suddenly the fire ceased. They
weren't sure if their positions had been compromised. Dave's team held
off on returning fire. Was the enemy shooting at them or not? They
didn't really know, because everyone out there still carried an AK-47,
so someone may have been shooting at a wild dog or something. With

no more fire, they proceeded to walk around for a few miles, without getting shot at, and got picked up by the HMMWVs again. They did a data dump of information they had collected for the Marines in the HMMWV so they could report it up the chain of command, and then the trucks dumped them off again in another area. And that's how it was for three days straight. Getting picked up, dropped off, no casualties, no shooting, just stealthily collecting information and reporting it.

Sniper teams are inserted and extracted in such a way as to conceal their activities and whereabouts. How they are able to do this is by syncing up with conventional forces in the area. For example, when Dave's team needed to be extracted from a particular area, they would radio the regular forces patrolling in the area so they could pull over at an exact location, get out to do a security haut, and then Dave's team would sync up with them covertly on the streets. Then they would all get back inside the HMMWV and drive off target. This is the same technique they used to get inserted in a particular location. As the HMMWV drove off target, Dave's team would unload the information until the next stop, where they would all get back out of the vehicle, but only the regular forces would return, while Dave's team would sneak off on foot under the cover of the natural and man-made terrain features around them. In theory, no one knew they were being dropped off. Then they would be on their own anywhere from forty-eight hours to ninety-six hours. To survive on their own for that amount of time, they carried everything they needed, which equaled a lot of weight. Dave carried an M16A4, thirteen magazines of roughly 360 rounds of ammunition, 200 rounds of ammunition for the SAW (the light machine gun), two or three hand grenades, two or three smoke grenades, a thermite grenade, a small amount of demolitions, usually some detonating cord and C4, two or three radio batteries, extra rounds for the sniper rifle, an M9 pistol and sixty rounds for the pistol, water, food, and a booby-trap kit. Everyone had their own load, but they were all usually carrying well over one hundred pounds of gear per person. Depending on the mission and the area, they would hunker down in various places for various amounts of time. Dave will never forget what happened during one particular time when he and the three other members of his sniper team were on the inside edge of Fallujah, concealed in bushes; it was a good position where they could hang out for a couple hours and get a shot off. It was one of the team members' time to rest, so he lay down on something and said, "I don't know what this is, but it's comfortable." It was pitch-dark out, so none of them could see what it was. When the sun started to come up the next morning, they saw what the guy had been sleeping on . . . he had been sleeping on a dead dog all night. Because everything smelled over there, they didn't notice the stench of its carcass. They left that spot soon after sunrise.

Sometimes they were able to find water pump houses or well houses to stay in overnight, and sometimes they just needed to commandeer someone's house. This was not uncommon. When they had to do this, his four-man team would come up to a courtyard wall (most houses in Iraq were surrounded by a courtyard and mud brick walls), and since Dave was the smallest guy on the team and was a gymnast when he was younger, he was always the first over the wall. His team members would toss him over the wall with his 9mm as fast as they could so he could open the courtyard gate and let the rest of the team into the courtyard before they let themselves into the house. He got good and comfortable being the first over the wall, so he always did it.

The first thing that goes through your head is, "Did anybody see me?" Then, "How the hell do I open the gate?" Once I got the guys in, we'd move all of our gear inside and close the gate as quietly as we could. We would try to open the door to the houses; we didn't kick the doors down. I got good at jimmying the locks and getting in. The occupants were usually sleeping in the house or on the roof in the summer, because they all had flat roofs and it was cooler up there. But in the winter we'd go in and try to figure out where the head of the house (male) was inside the house. We would wake him up at gunpoint. We would tell him, in our horrible Arabic, "Wake up your family, and we are going to move them all into one room. We are not here to hurt you, but your house is ours now, and if you try anything, we'll kill all of you." I know it sounds barbaric, but this is at a time when you couldn't trust anyone, and no matter what you were, if you were in a U.S. military uniform, you were being shot at. Oh, and being a sniper meant you usually had a bounty on your head anyway. We would stay there as long as we needed, usually until nightfall, with at least one of us having constant watch over the family. Once we needed to leave, we would call for an extract. Because the family would spread the news that we were there as soon as we left, that entire area would become unsafe for us. We would throw a smoke grenade if we had to meet up with the vehicle. After three or four days out on our own, we were pretty beat down, supplies were low, and we were hungry."

Dave tried to eat what the locals ate. "They were skinny dudes who could run, jump in sandals, so they were doing something right; they were eating stuff that gave them the energy." Dave kept a journal of recipes he picked up from eating the local food, which he enjoyed. He ate a lot of rice with short-grain pasta in it, mixed with raisins or chopped-up dates, a lot of chicken, yogurt, round flat bread, a lot of potatoes and tomato-based products, ground beef in fried dough, goat, and cucumbers. The Euphrates ran close by, so there was a lot of vegetation, and crops grew well. There was a good amount of farmland and a decent amount of food to eat.

The coolest mission I went on, I don't remember if was a week and a half or two weeks, we were out, but we linked up with a company and we pretty much became forward scouts for them. We would go into an area looking for IEDs and whatever other sort of trouble was around. We were given free rein. The company didn't have a mission per se for us; all they wanted us to do was to push forward to find safe locations for the company to sleep at night and just sort of sneak around scouting the area. So we were essentially freelance scouts. I have pictures of the four of us in the middle of nowhere; we look like nomads, just wandering about (of course, stealthily). We gathered a lot of intelligence in those weeks; the Company detained a lot of people and answered a lot of priority intelligence requirements, and we never took any shots.

WHAT'S DIFFERENT ABOUT US?

"What's different about sniper platoons is that each one is set up slightly different and is unique to the people in the team. It's not like the rest of the Marine Corps, where if you are in a rifle company you know what happens in a rifle company in another battalion; you have the same mission and composition. This is not the case in sniper platoons." Sniper platoons run four- and five-man teams; some even break down further into two-man teams. There are even different weapons used and assigned among the teams. What makes a sniper platoon unique and special is that the individuals on the teams are hand selected. Snipers don't get assigned to a sniper team the way infantry Marines get assigned to a rifle company. Snipers know who they are going to be assigned with and why. After you indoc into the sniper platoon, which is basically like a draft, the team leaders hand select who they want on their platoons and teams. They handcraft the teams by knowing what each individual brings to the team, both personally and professionally. Dave states that because the teams are hand selected, there were never any real personality clashes. If problems came up among them, they were able to sit down and hash them out fairly quickly with no long-term consequences. This relationship is further enforced within the teams because the team members usually do not wear rank, and they were all on a first-name basis. "No one was 'above' anyone else." Of course, if they were back in the rear and had to do a dog-and-pony show, they assumed and wore their rank and titles, but after that, they went back to being Joe, Bob, Tom, etc. When they were on a field operation, every team member had a say. Even though the senior guy would ultimately enforce the command, the junior guys could voice their concerns about it. They all contributed their opinions, and they were all asked for them, because their ultimate goal was to not get killed. "If any one of us on a team gets killed, the probability of another team member getting killed is high. We have no backup; we back each other up." Dave says sometimes they got on each other's nerves, just like your friends and family do, and they would fight. Once he got in a fistfight with a team member and lost horribly. And a week before this interview with him, years after this fight, the guy he lost to spent the weekend with Dave at his home, hanging out, drinking beer, and having a good time. "Nobody from outside the teams or platoons dared confront us. We were a band of brothers, just like the entire Marine Corps, and if an outsider challenged or provoked one of us, they would get the wrath of the entire team, or platoon."

THERE'S FALLUJAH, THEN THERE'S *CAMP FALLUJAH*

As a sniper, Dave worked for the conventional forces battalion, so technically, he did not fall under Special Operations Command (SOCOM).

Even though sniper schools are "special operations" schools and every-thing snipers do makes them "special operations" capable, they techni-cally are not Special Operations, nor do they fall under the command and control of SOCOM. "So by the rules it puts us in a gray area. Even though we can be directly attached to Special Operations Forces (SOF), we were not SOF. Does that make sense? I was attached to a SEAL team once for a month. And even though we had gone through similar training and conducted ourselves operationally the same, we were not SOF, and they had cooler gear and equipment than us. When I first was attached to the SEAL team, I thought, I can't wait to see these guys in action!" But at the end of the day he realized they were doing the same TTPs (tactics, techniques, and procedures) as he did, and he thought, "We're not that different. Although they would beat my ass in the water any day." Luckily, he was in the desert. "So what does that make me? I went to a Special Operations School, I support Special Operations as an asset, but I'm not Special Operations. I don't know where I fall." A common question of Marine Scout Snipers.

Dave says there's a huge rivalry between infantry and non-infantry Marines. "All snipers come from the infantry. Snipers and infantry all go through the same training; initially, it's those of us who want to push ourselves to get selected into a more specialized school who go on to become snipers. Yes, snipers carry cooler gear and have more free-dom to operate independently, sometimes with no oversight, but there wasn't a rift between snipers and infantry. I would say the bigger rift was between staff NCOs (noncommissioned officers) and us (snipers). We were considered to be more of subject-matter experts (SMEs) than they were, and it pissed some of them off." When Dave's team had to stay with the infantry, they were their guests. Dave's team knew most of them personally, and they liked having snipers alongside them because they were an asset to the infantry; in turn, the snipers liked having the infantry close by because when they got into a "shit sandwich," there was somebody around with a lot more firepower. So there was really no rift between the sniper teams and infantry; the rift was between infantry and non-infantry.

This may sound trivial, but it's something that drives us (snipers and in-fantry) insane. Fallujah and Al Anbar were bad, dangerous areas. There were just always a lot of people getting killed; we were basically on the front lines of it all. You see people being blown up and shot, enemy and friendly, it's just the way it was. The city proper was very small, about three to four miles wide. It's a very dense city, but not a large city; it was definitely not as big as Washington, D.C. Camp Baharia was just outside of Fallujah, where the battalion in charge of the city was located. That was a relatively safe camp. But then you had Camp Fallujah, the largest base in the area. From what I understand, it actually encompassed more area than the city of Fallujah did. It was insanely big. So they operated like a normal base with morale boosters like USO shows, organized runs, and all sorts of dumb contests. They had an awesome chow hall, and everyone had to wear rank and blouse their pants with boot bands, you know, normal Marine Corps base activity, but in a war zone. When we came back from our missions, we didn't think we were hot shit by any means; heck, we didn't even run into that much combat. But when we would talk to people after we returned home from deployment and I would tell them I was in Fallujah, they would say, "Oh, me too." It was nice, because you could talk to them about something you had in common, something that others might not understand, so it was nice to have others to talk about the shit you saw and had to live through. I would say, "Oh, you must remember the blue mosque . . ."; everyone who is anyone operating in Fallujah knows about the blue mosque. Whenever you passed by it, you got shot at, no matter what time of year, day, etc. And then they would say, "No, I was at Camp Fallujah, I was never outside the wire in the city." Dudes would go there for a year and never leave the camp. I would think, wow, how could they have been for a year and never leave the camp, never see the "real" Fallujah? The surgical center was at Camp Fallujah, so all wounded went there. One particular day I remember we were out and some guys got wounded, and it was faster to get the wounded to Camp Fallujah Surgical than be medevaced out by a helo. We were all piled in a truck, and the guys driving the truck drove straight through the main gate to Camp Fallujah. They weren't hauling ass, but they were driving with a purpose; we had to get to the surgical center. It was standard operating procedures at the time that all vehicles entering Camp Fallujah had to stop and all persons inside had to clear their weapons before being let through. Well, we didn't do that. We radioed the gate to tell them we had wounded and we breezed through, obviously thinking it was okay because lives were at stake. As we are passing through, this female Marine lieutenant, who is running in PT gear no less, is trying to flag our vehicle down to make us slow down on base. She had no concept that there was a war going on outside the gates of that base. While people are out there getting shot up, she's running in PT gear, yelling at us to slow down! That aggravated me. It seemed some people stationed there were more focused on PT and parties than the war that was going on around them. And these are the same people who come back and thump their chests while saying that they were in Fallujah during the war. While they were being entertained by USO shows, we would be running extra missions because they didn't want the base getting attacked during the show. And we did so gladly, that's what we signed up to do, but then they turn around and yell at us for driving too fast on base to get to the surgical center to save a guy's leg. Pathetic.

YOU'RE NOT ALLOWED TO EAT IN MY CHOW HALL

"I remember one mission that we were sent on, with a twenty-minute notice, which was an absolute cluster fuck, and what happened after was a kick in the teeth. We were sent out in the middle of nowhere, somewhere outside Fallujah, I really don't remember the exact location, which took us forever to get to, to babysit this bridge because intelligence reporting said something was going to happen. We were out there for a week, and all we saw the entire time was one dude taking a shit, I kid you not. I was on the gun, dialing in on this one dude as he's getting close to the bridge, and then he drops his pants and does his business." Dave's team was out there for approximately five to seven days, which he said felt like forever. It was just the four of them living in a hole. They stunk like shit. They had gone out totally sanitized, meaning they didn't wear nametapes or rank insignia, nor did they carry Geneva Conventions cards.

We were told go out with nothing, so we did; But that wasn't the real reason. We weren't doing covert operations; the real reason why we were sanitized was because if something happened to one of us while we were out there, our families wouldn't see it on the news first, they would be notified appropriately before they'd see their son's dead body being desecrated by insurgents on the 6 p.m. news. If we carried ID cards, the enemy would know who we were and take advantage of it by disgracing us and parading our bodies on TV for propaganda before our families could be notified that we had been killed in action. We didn't want to be cowboys; we wanted to protect our kin. Nevertheless, we had to explain this to the regular forces every time we were seen on Camp Fallujah without our ID cards. We're snipers; we already had bounties on our heads.

At the time of this bridge-watching mission, Dave's sniper team's parent command hadn't deconflicted their mission and presence with the other operating forces in the area. So there they were, in a concealed position and unrecognizable because they were covered in mud, just the four of them, with no way of distinguishing that they were even U.S. citizens, aside from their nice white teeth. As they were watching the bridge, waiting for any type of action, they saw a Cobra come over them; a U.S.-owned attack helicopter. There were initially excited because there wasn't supposed to be anything out there, so at least they could "roll tach" (change the radio frequency so they could talk to air). He kept circling them. And then he started tilting. Dave thought, "Oh shit, we are being targeted by our own forces! I thought, we should have probably put out some air panels right now. He was tilting, so we didn't know if he was going to start a gun run or what. We later found out they didn't know we were there, and they spotted us and were targeting us! So we threw out air panels, which were big orange sheets of plastic cloth to signal to them that we were not the enemy." (You can put air panels on anything that needs to be identified from the air to signal aircraft.) Can you imagine getting shot by one of your own because of a lack of deconfliction? Unfortunately, it happens, and it wasn't the first time it happened to Dave's sniper team. Fortunately, they didn't get shot, and the Cobra saw the air panels.

Aside from the guy taking a shit and the Cobra targeting us, at the end of those 5–7 days we saw nothing, we accomplished nothing. So when we got picked up, we were taken to Camp Fallujah to get something hot to eat. Mind you, five to seven days living on MREs and water rations; that means no showering, no shaving. We stunk, we looked like hell, we had tons of facial growth, our hair was long, we were dirty, but above all, we were hungry. We were so excited that we were going to Camp Fallujah to eat. It had been almost three months since we had a real meal. We got to the gate, and this time we cleared and cleaned our weapons. Our weapons are an extension of us; we are nothing without them, so we take excellent care of them. We go to the chow hall, and we are denied access because we didn't have our ID cards. Remember, we went out sanitized, meaning there was nothing on us that could give away our identities; we were ghosts out there. Our hearts sank. We just wanted this one small pleasure. So a USMC captain sees us and vouches for us and gets us into the chow hall. We all got our food, sat down, and start eating. As we ate, we began to realize that food was something we had taken for granted, because we were so thankful for it. All of a sudden we start to notice everyone who is sitting around us is getting up and leaving. We just looked at them wondering what's going on? What don't we know? We didn't care, we continued to enjoy the food. About ten minutes go by, and a different USMC officer comes up to us and says that we are too dirty to be eating in his chow hall. He made us leave the chow hall. At least he allowed us to take our food and finish eating outside. We felt humiliated; we had been treated like dogs. Unfortunately, that became a common experience for us. Like I said earlier, they had no idea what a war really was, the dirty stench of war. I wanted to tell him, "This is what guys who fight the war look like, and you won't let us eat in your chow hall!?" He even had the audacity to ask us why we didn't shave. Let's see, because one gallon of water weighs eight pounds. I drink a gallon a day and I'm out for four days. That means technically I'd have to carry thirty-two pounds of water, and I can't do that. All I can carry is about three gallons, so I can carry everything else to stay alive. So maybe he could understand why I'm not wasting any of my water to shave when I'm out in the field. We continually had to explain this to people. Water was a big issue, and we were told we just had to plus up on water to survive out there, but we simply couldn't. It weighed too much.

CONDITIONED TO WAR

Dave remembers coming off a mission with his team inside the city of Fallujah, and an infantry squad came by to pick them up. The infantry squad was out doing "presence patrols," a show of force to let the locals in the area know they were in the area and of course observing them and all activities going on. The squad just happened to walk by the house Dave and his teammates were staying in, albeit as uninvited guests, and they walked out the front door as the squad passed by and fell in right behind them. He said he was sure everybody knew what they were doing and that they had just come from that house, but at least they had protection. The squad was going to escort them back to the center of the city where the government center was, the large compound he thinks was called the "CMUC" (pronounced *see-muck*) but he can't remember what it stands for, where U.S. forces were staying. Before entering friendly lines into the CMUC you always had to request permission via radio. "As we walked up to the gate, we were on foot, not in a vehicle. Someone in the squad saw something that looked suspicious. It was a dead dog with what appeared to be wires coming out of it. So instead of asking permission to enter, he radioed the CMUC to tell them that there was a possible IED in the area. No sooner did he say, 'Be advised there's a dog that appears to have wires . . . ,' over the radio, when Ka-Boom! The dog blew up! And without missing a beat he picks up where he left off: 'Never mind, request permission to enter friendly lines.' The dog blew up, before he could even finish calling in the suspected IED. Using dead dogs as IED was popular back then. But that's how it was, you get conditioned to war and it conditions you. You just got used to things that would be horrific here, but there, it was just another day." And for those animal lovers, like myself, who are cringing while reading this, Dave tells me that these were not dogs that you have as household pets; they were wild, vicious, and mostly rabid dogs that would attack. It doesn't make it a whole lot easier to swallow, but a little bit easier.

"SS" BOLTS

Dave returned from deployment after seven months. He got back and was sent to a lot of schools: Combat Marksmanship Instructor; SERE (Survival, Evasion, Resistance, and Escape) School (where he turned twenty years old, still not old enough to legally drink); Mountain Scout Sniper School; Desert Warfare training. He postponed predeployment leave so he could go to Urban Scout Sniper School with Special Operations Training Group. Then he went back over to the sandbox for his second deployment to Fallujah in 2007. This time Dave led a five-man sniper team. Their weapons were different; they had some experimental weapons. Dave carried the XM3 short bolt-action 308, Mark 11 (MK11), which were all suppressed, 308s, M107s, and M40a3s. The gear had really changed in one year. But what hadn't changed was that one year later he found himself in the same hooch that still had the "SS" symbol that his previous sniper team spray-painted on it a year earlier.

So back at the same hooch a year later, Dave said the vibe was different this time. They knew it was going to be a lot more relaxed this deployment; not necessarily less dangerous, but fewer combat engagements. The forces there had done a great job keeping ordnance out of the city, so the IEDs were less dangerous because they were made more from homemade explosives now rather than ordnance. The most prominent IED makers had already been targeted and killed. Attacks were on a smaller scale, and overall things seemed to be getting safer. They still dealt with serious casualties, guys losing limbs and bleeding out. During one attack Dave had become the guy in charge of the observation post, and somehow he became in charge of a squad. He didn't know the guys. They were from another company, but because he had more stripes on his arm than anybody else there and the guys that were his senior were lying on the ground bleeding, he had to jump up and assume the position of squad leader, as well as team leader. "I got indoctrinated pretty quickly."

FALLUJAH 2007, PINNED DOWN IN AN AMBUSH ATTACK

You know on his previous deployment Dave had become the first guy over the wall because of his stature and his physical aptitude. So this time around he kept it up and was still the first guy over the wall. "I wanted to be. I didn't want these guys to get killed, and I really didn't want to have to explain to their parents why they weren't coming back. So I'd rather take the risk of being the first over. I was twenty years old at that time. I was in charge of the team, but I wasn't the oldest."

He'll never forget one combat mission during this deployment:

It was the craziest thing that happened to me, even though it's just a typical day in the life of a sniper. I wanted my team to get some rest, so I left them in the rear and went out with a platoon that was going into an area I wanted to survey to find out how my team could sneak in at night and do our thing in the near future. So I asked the platoon if I could tag along. We were in the city proper and my team was at Baharia, and all of a sudden we started hearing a lot of chatter over the radios, then gunfire and explosions. I could hear the stress in people's voices on the radios. We find out a MTT (Military Transition Team), who were training the Iraqi Army, were getting attacked about four hundred yards away. It was afternoon, and we made our way to their location. We weren't prepared to see what we saw when we arrived on target. You know it's a bad scene when you see an M4 that's been blown in half, flak jackets littering the street covered in blood, and pockmarks everywhere from hand grenades. I saw one dude huddled and crying in front of a vehicle, the one vehicle that got hit and got separated from rest of the convoy. This guy turned out to be a major, who got a Bronze Star out of it, go figure, but there is no fire at this point. Everything has stopped for the moment. There is a lieutenant in the back of the HMMWV that the major is huddled in front of who is dead. I found out he got shot by an enemy sniper. Later we found out the entire ambush was initiated by that sniper. Some of the guys were trying to get the major to tell them what had happened, but he was shell-shocked. All he could tell us was that they were ambushed and took fire from all directions. No sooner does he relay this, we start getting lit up. There are four medium machine guns that had us in a crossfire ambushing the shit out of us from elevated positions. They were on top of a building, and they had us pinned down at this point. There were a lot of them. I was firing my M4 on semiautomatic, and I was running out of ammunition; I had 360 rounds with me. Because of the way the ambush was set up and the position of the vehicles, this particular vehicle can't turn around and get off the target. We have dead and wounded, and I ran out of 5.56mm ammunition in seven minutes. The five of us were pinned down in this street just watching the enemy pop up through my iron sights, and we're shooting back. Not good.

Dave kept tracer rounds at the bottom of his last three or four magazines to alert himself that he would run out of ammunition soon. He was shooting his 556 at targets popping up from a wall about twelve feet away, and the rounds were just skipping off the top of the wall because it was so thick, and the tracers were burning out. At this point he thought to himself, "I have to try to keep the heads down of the enemy so we can get the wounded out. I've got no more ammo, and I just can't sit here waiting to get shot." So he gave his rifle to his friend Chuck and told the guys to lay down cover fire for him while he advanced forward without any cover. For some reason he was the only one who had some hand grenades, so the only thing he knew he could do and had to do was try to take out the enemy machine gun positions with his hand grenades. "The first thing you learn about hand grenades is to never throw a hand grenade up. But in this situation, I either throw the hand grenade up, or die. The choice was easy." So he ran up to the twelve-foot wall and tossed a grenade up over the wall onto the roof. It ended up knocking out one of the machine guns. Fire ceased just long enough for them to throw some smoke grenades, get into the vehicles, and get everyone off the ambush site. He got a Navy and Marine Corps Achievement Medal (NAM) with a V (the V device is a miniature bronze or gold letter V that stands for combat valor) for that day.

Dave was modest as he explained how the remaining survivors and deceased all got out of there because everyone did what they were trained to do. All he did was throw the hand grenade that ceased fire long enough for them to buy the time they needed to do what they all were trained to do, and that's how they all got off the target. But he ran out in the middle of an ambush scene, with minimal cover fire, remember they were all running out of ammo, and used his hand grenades in a most unconventional way. But that's war. They do what they are trained to do and think on their feet and react accordingly. The crazy part about it was he just happened to ask to go with this platoon to do a recon mission for his team. They just happened to be in the area where this ambush had taken place, and he just happened to be able to support during the ambush.

We get trained on how to not wander into an ambush. We know what to do and what not to do, but there were Marines out there who needed saving, so you go into the situation no matter what, you want them to do the same for you if those actions lead to an ambush. By all the signs it was the quintessential ambush pattern. The hit vehicle was in an alleyway, basically a cross street that wasn't wide enough to where you could turn a HMMWV around; you couldn't fit two HMMWVs side by side. If you think about how the dimensions of the HMMWV came about, they are built as wide as they can be to be able to get through the narrowest alleyway in Europe. In retrospect we should have known the enemy was waiting for the first responders to get to the hit vehicle, and it was an ambush just waiting to happen, but when you are in it, you only think, those are our friends, they are Marines, and they are wounded. You don't give a shit what could happen; you go in there and help them.

Without the mental and emotional capacity to make a split-second decision while his life and the lives of others are on the line, and without the courage to trust his ability, perhaps Dave wouldn't have followed his gut instinct to run the gauntlet of fire and do what he thought was the only hope of getting those people out safely that day. Perhaps I would have never gotten the chance to interview him and share his story with you. Thankfully, he did follow his gut instinct and trusted his years of training and a year of combat experience, gained all before the ripe ol' age of twenty-one, and is alive today to talk about it.

LOOKING BACK

As Dave looked back at his career as a young Scout Sniper, he told me that he misses his brothers. The sense of pride he had as a sniper could never be matched by anything else. He reveals he didn't have to leave a wife and kids at home, and this made him lucky and unlucky at the same time. "Sometimes I used to think my courage under fire would prove my manliness and make me worthy of a woman. I know now those were silly thoughts, but back then, they were pretty serious, as I desperately wanted to find companionship, especially hearing about the girlfriends and wives of others back home. I had no one to talk about, to go home to. It made me bitter back then, but I have learned that if you are true to yourself good things will come. I was truly the best sniper I could be, and good things have come from that." Dave is still young, but he's lived twice his years, and one day he'll find a person to share the rest of his years with, maybe taking a little advantage of some frivolous fun he missed out on while in combat before the legal drinking age as a Marine Corps Scout Sniper.

3

DOING GOD'S WORK

In December 2003, Sonny graduated from the 1st Marine Division (MARDIV) Scout Sniper Basic Course (SSBC). It was one of the toughest, most demanding schools he ever attended at the time and one of the biggest accomplishments of his life. "This school is everything to a Marine in an infantry battalion; this was the pinnacle for grunts. Not only was it physically demanding, but it was mentally challenging, and exhausting. The written tests were the toughest part. Everything was expected to be memorized verbatim." Sonny came from an infantry battalion, so he was expected to already be up to speed on the definitions and common knowledge associated with being a sniper. But he had only been in the sniper platoon for three months before he went to SSBC, so he didn't have the time to memorize all the definitions and terms verbatim. He was also busy stalking, shooting, learning the radios, making field-expedient antennae, etc. Even so, he failed only one test, Mission Planning, but he retook it and passed.

> I'm not the brightest, but I'm not the dumbest. We volunteer to take the indoc so the leadership in the sniper platoon can see if we have what it takes to just be in the platoon. I knew it was going to be challenging, but that's why you join the Marine Corps. I also knew this was what I wanted. At the time I indoc'd, 1st Battalion/5th Marines (1/5) had lost

a lot of HOGs; some got out, some switched duty stations after the Iraq invasion in March 2003, so they needed to refill the ranks with men from the STA Platoon. Once you are accepted into the STA Platoon, you start learning all of the knowledge that is associated with being a sniper. You really become a professional. To me it was the equivalent of a master's degree for grunts. You're expected to know so much, and you do. Men that attended SSBC coming from a recon battalion, force recon battalion, or now from MARSOC don't, to my knowledge, take an indoc just to be able to go to this school. They go to get more training, hone the skills they already have, and to earn another MOS. For those guys who attend, it's usually who the best shot on the team is, who has the time, who wants it, or who is told to go by their chiefs because a sniper team needs a sniper. They are given the definitions and the rest of the knowledge they need to be successful at the course, and they usually are, because they already have specialized training and are already doing cool shit. To them it is simply put, "another tool for the tool bag." These guys are already vetted and "high-speed." But for an infantry Marine in an infantry battalion . . . this is the coolest shit, this is the top.

Growing up, Sonny was one of those guys you would picture becoming a sniper. He was born in Jackson, Mississippi, in 1981. His parents divorced when he was about two years old. His mom remarried, and they moved to the Delta: Indianola, Mississippi, to be precise. Hunting and fishing became a lifestyle for Sonny while in the Delta. His stepfather taught him to hunt and fish, but he never taught him how to shoot, with precision at least. He would tell Sonny, "Here's a gun. This is how you aim at your target; don't jerk the trigger." That was pretty much the extent of it. He learned to shoot a Red Ryder BB gun first. He would play around in the backyard, shooting blackbirds, which was "ok" with his mother and grandmother because "they were a nuisance, but if they ever found out he took target practice at squirrels, blue jays, robins, or cardinals, they would have had his hide! For Sonny, though, they were all there for his target practice.

Finally the day came when he was old enough to own his first *real* gun; he was seven years old. It was an H&R, 20 gauge, single shot. He was so excited—he felt like a *real* man now. That was until he shot the gun for the very first time and cried like a little girl. "It kicked my ass. It shook me up; I was so upset." His stepfather, whom we'll call Chester, set a beer can on the ground about ten feet away. "Ok, son . . . shoot it." Sonny thought, "Easy enough! This target isn't even moving like the blackbirds; I got this." Sonny is not a physically overbearing man; in fact, he's always been smaller than most guys his age. He positioned himself with his back about two feet in front of the rear tire of Chester's truck, sighted in, took a deep breath, held it in ("not what you're supposed to do, but with a shotgun and only ten yards from the target with birdshot . . . not a big deal"), and fired! That low brass birdshot kicked his ass, especially because he was a smaller guy. The recoil sent him flying back into Chester's truck. "That's why I cried. It scared the shit outta me and knocked me back into the truck's wheel well. That was my first lesson in recoil. But I hit the beer can!" After the initial shock wore off, he stopped crying. And after he stopped crying, Sonny realized he had just found his new passion and wasn't about to let his smaller-than-average male physique get in the way. Seeing Sonny's potential, and his enthusiasm, Chester bought him another gun, an H&R 4-10 that wasn't as heavy and had less recoil. Sonny was ecstatic; he owned two guns, and he wasn't even a teenager yet.

After Chester and his mom divorced, Sonny and his mother moved all around the U.S. for the next two years and eventually wound up back in Mississippi, but this time he was in the hills, in a small town called Amory (pronounced *aim-ree*). He was attending high school with no thoughts or desires of continuing on to college. He had been thinking about the military. He always knew he wanted to join; it was a calling. He had always looked up to his grandfather, who had retired from the Navy and was a devout Southern Baptist who operated straight out of the Bible.

I am the total opposite of him in a lot of ways, not that I'm an atheist or hoodlum, but I certainly was not as into the Bible as he was. I'm also a lot smaller in stature than he was, and I went into the Marine Corps; he was in the Navy. I'll never forget this one story he told me about when he went to get his first tattoo; it was either in Korea or Vietnam. He told me he went out drinking with guys (he doesn't drink), and they all ended up at a tattoo parlor. He sat down in the chair and was going to get his first tattoo; that is, until the tip of the tattoo gun touched his hand. He jumped up out of the chair and said, "Nope, you're not touching me with that gun!" My grandfather was a big man, and he wasn't letting that tattoo gun get near him again. He refused to pay the guy for his time and walked out. And look at me . . . I'm covered in tats! We were the opposite in so many ways, but even so, I admired him so much, and I wanted to emulate him. I've always been independent, and I chose my own path as far as the military went.

Prior to graduating from high school in 1999, Sonny joined the Mississippi National Guard, with parental consent, in November 1998, while in his senior year. After graduation he left for boot camp on June 2, 1999. Near the end of September he graduated from Fort Knox, Kentucky, as an M1A1 Crewman. This was his first introduction to real marksmanship. "Shooting out to 300 meters, I was horrible. I didn't possess the fundamentals or patience. Granted it was the Army, sorry guys, and their marksmanship at Fort Knox was lacking a little. We were training to become tankers; using the 120mm smoothbore cannon, two-240s, and a .50 cal. Seriously . . . why would rifle marksmanship be that big of a deal? At that point I was certain I was destined to just be a marksman or sharpshooter, never expecting years later I'd earn the title 'sniper.'"

While he was in boot camp for the National Guard at Fort Knox, Sonny's barracks were adjacent to the Marines' barracks. He would see them in the chow hall line and in the motor pool training getting smoked. "Our Army instructors who were training us would say, 'Those Marines are the shit.' Back then I thought, what's the difference? We basically wear the same uniform." After basic training he ended up attended a local community college in the fall of 2000, because he still wanted to play soccer. "In high school I just wanted to mess around in the woods, hunt, fish. I wasn't really interested in girls, but that changed when I went to college. [He was a late bloomer.] Even so, I dropped out after soccer season. I went ADSW [Active Duty for Special Work] for a few months for the Guard and attended a leadership course with the Army, then got my conditional release to join the Marines." He didn't even finish the first semester before he quit and followed his calling; he joined the Marine Corps. Three of his friends in college had been discussing joining, and that put the bug in his ear. He remembered observing the Marines at Fort Knox and how the Army instructors talked about them and decided he was ready for something different in his life. So he decided he would go with his three friends to the Marine Corps recruiter. After six months of waiting for conditional-release paperwork from the Guard unit he was still in (conditional-release paperwork allows you to switch from one branch of the Armed Forces to another without losing time), his battalion commander signed his release. On the day after, August 20, 2001, he left for Marine Corps Recruit Depot (MCRD) in San Diego.

Sonny joined the Marines as an infantryman. Three weeks after he arrived at MCRD San Diego, 9/11 happened.

I didn't see the first plane hit the tower, but one of my drill instructors, Staff Sergeant KB, called me into the duty hut early in the morning and told me to sit down. I remember hearing him yell, "Guide, get in here!" That was meant for me. I hustled over. "Recruit Sonny reporting as ordered, Sir!" And then I watched in astonishment as the second plane struck the tower. I didn't know what it meant. I was a twenty-year-old guy, barely a man, with no worries about life or war. The only stress I had at that point was being constantly yelled at to do something that certainly wasn't life threatening—more annoying, really. Drill Sergeant KB was this huge black dude who was ripped. He wasn't a POG [a slang term that stands for People Other than Grunts], he was infantry and then went on to be a sniper. He was in Somalia in '92 or '93, before Black Hawk Down. He had a combat action ribbon; he was the real deal. He told me it was an attack on the United States and then asked me what my MOS (military occupational specialty) was. My response, with a shit-eating grin, was "Infantry." He said, "Good. You'll be going to war soon."

Drill Sergeant KB was the dude I talked to who inspired me years later to go to D.C. years after my combat deployments. I was young, I had just done two back-to-back combat deployments, and I felt I needed a break; I couldn't have been more wrong. The only two good things I got out of D.C. were my son, Jackson, and my TS SCI. I got in more trouble there, because it just wasn't my thing. I started drinking a lot while in D.C. because all my friends were deploying and doing cool shit and I wasn't. They were taking the fight to those assholes, and I was riding a desk, stuck in D.C. doing presidential support duty. So I went back to doing cool shit again after that and have been doing it ever since.

Sonny graduated from boot camp on November 16, 2001, which is around the time when everything was kicking off in Afghanistan. He didn't go straight to war after boot camp. He attended and graduated from School of Infantry (SOI) West in January 2002 and was stationed at Camp San Mateo in Alpha Company, 1st Battalion, 5th Marines (1/5). He ended up getting into "O" Company because of his excellent swim qualifications. After Boat Company training in Coronado and CAGS (combined armed exercise) in Twentynine Palms, it would be time to go to war.

OFF TO INVADE IRAQ: 2003

February 2003 rolled around, and Sonny, who was an infantry team leader at the time, not a sniper, was on his way to the sandbox; first stop, Kuwait. He sat in Kuwait desert training for a month and half before they got the call to go into Iraq. U.S. forces invaded Iraq on March 20, 2003.

> My platoon commander, 2nd Platoon, Alpha Company 1/5, got killed on March 23rd, the morning we crossed the LOD (line of departure; the line designated to attack from). He was a pretty cool motherfucker. He was a mustang and went to The Citadel. He got his degree, went through the USMC Officer Candidate School and The Basic School (OCS/TBS), then came to the fleet. He was all about his Marines; he was a great leader. It sucked that he got killed. We were at Gas Oil Separation Plant (GOSP) 2. Alpha Company was tasked with seizing GOSP2 and the southern Rumaila oil fields. Artillery was prepping the target, GOSP2, the night before moving to contact. That morning we cleared some rock quarries. Nothing was there, so we pushed toward the main objective, GOSP2. As we got to the objective, you could hear guys fragging the shit out of every-thing. This was everyone's first taste of war, except for a few of the older guys. There was a Gunny with us; he was a bad dude, awesome, who was a Ranger in Panama or Grenada, I can't remember, who did four years as a Ranger, got out, and then joined the Marine Corps. He was our company Gunny. He got killed later in Baghdad. So we're clearing our objective and we reach our LOA (limit of advance), which was a road facing east, as the sun was just coming up. We have snipers attached to us, (snipers are badass). They are on our left and right flanks and amtracks in front of the 31s (31 is short for the MOS 0331, Machine Gunner), which are our machine gunners who are attached to us with their 240s (machine gun). We are looking out toward the LOA, right to left, with the sun in

our eyes, and you start seeing people in the distance about 250 yards away, peeking over piles of rubble. I remember this was the first time I saw the enemy in a combat situation, and their heads looked huge, like alien heads. In my mind it was like, "Holy Shit!" We consolidated on a road off to the south, which ran on an N-S axis. There was a technical on this road; a term for an enemy vehicle. It was an Isuzu pickup minus the machine gun mounted in the back. That son of a bitch starts hauling ass north, and we hear it over the radio, and everyone is taking cover, getting into prone facing the technical. I can see the driver bending down behind the wheel to protect himself from our fire as he's driving by shooting at us. Nobody opened fire until that guy did; we waited, and then we shot him up like Swiss cheese, but he still drove off. However, right before we returned fire, our lieutenant, who hears the gunfire, stands up and walks out between the amtracks and gets shot under his flak. He went into shock and died later. He was the first KIA for coalition forces, to my knowledge, for Operation Iraqi Freedom. In our minds, after our AAR (after action report), everyone was really emotional, and we are thinking, "Why the fuck did no one shoot earlier? Why did we wait?" We all heard it being called over the ISR (infantry squad radio); we knew it was coming. Another vehicle tried to do the same thing shortly after. He didn't make it like the other one did; he got dead real fast. But when you think about the situation with the lieutenant, you know the sniper had a split-second decision to make, so you wonder if he pulled the trigger, would that lieutenant have died? Looking back, that incident was one of the major inspirations for me wanting to become a sniper and just watching them in combat. Knowing that they can turn a battle in a heartbeat. One sniper can dictate the battle and how enemy forces maneuver. Knowing that, did it for me. As for why that sniper didn't fire that day, you don't know. We all left the scene emotionally distraught. We all looked up to him because of the knowledge he brought.

On April 9th (2003) we get to Sadr City, outside of Baghdad. We stayed in a city dump, no shit; no pun intended there. There were rats everywhere; it was horrible. The next morning we roll into the city itself and I am in the worst firefight I had ever been in. There were RPGs and shit everywhere. I'm not gonna lie, it was . . . it was different. It was weird. Ya know.

As Sonny began to tell me this story, he paused and looked up a lot, recalling the information as if he was looking at the horrific mental images of the fight that day. I read body language, and I'm considered to be a "body language expert," but I didn't have to be an expert to know from his facial expressions, eye movements, and body language that those events are still hard to swallow to this day. And no, I don't know what it's like. In fact, I can't even imagine what he saw or how he felt, or the long-lasting effects it has left on him. I can empathize with him and picture war movies I've seen in my mind, trying to re-create a scene that could have looked like what he witnessed that day, but I don't know what it must have been like; I'll never know. "Our Gunny ended up getting killed. He was in a thin-skinned vehicle. [A thin-skinned vehicle refers to a HMMWV with no armor protecting it.] His driver got shot in the hand and it came out his elbow, and the Gunny was calling in the medevac for his driver when he got shot. I remember when the Gunny got killed, the driver, who had been shot too, jumped out of his HMMWV and jumped into our amtrack yelling, 'Gunny's dead, Gunny's dead!' And everybody was like holy fuck. Because the company Gunny in a Marine Corps battalion is revered, he is idolized, more so than the first sergeant. That was a devastating blow. We cleared a mosque and then ended up at the Presidential Palace, and then we were there for a few days before we went down to Diwaniya. We stayed there a few days, and then we were sent back home." Sonny got back to the States and attended the funeral processions, the first time he had ever had to do that. The 1/5 Battalion had three Killed in Action (KIA) and lots of Wounded in Action (WIA).

"Alpha 1/5 had to be one of the best-trained companies for the invasion. We got tasked with a lot of shit. And to my knowledge, 1/5 was the tip of the spear for where we went through the breach at in Iraq, so that was pretty cool." As you will read in the next story, told by a Marine Corps Scout Sniper who was also invading Iraq along with Sonny, albeit in a separate battalion with a separate mission, they were indeed the tip of the spear.

THE COOLEST JOB IN THE MARINE CORPS: SCOUT SNIPER

While Sonny was transferred to 1st Platoon from 2nd Platoon, he found out the Battalion STA Platoon was going to run an indoc. The STA

Platoon in the Marine Corps works directly for the S-2 (Intelligence section) and conducts reconnaissance, surveillance, and any other type of intelligence collection, but most importantly, the STA Platoon is the home of Marine Corps Scout Snipers. Sonny wanted to indoc for STA Platoon in the worst way.

> I got moved from 2nd Platoon to 1st Platoon. I was the 1st Squad Leader and pretty senior in the platoon. We had been training for two months in basic infantry tactics, basic grunt shit, but I wanted to indoc. The new boot lieutenant of 1st Platoon, who I don't even think had any combat experience then, tells me I can't go. I had to force my way to indoc and deceive him by telling him I just wanted to see if I could get selected, knowing (and praying) that I would get selected because I wanted it so bad. Sure enough, I was selected, and once I got into the platoon (STA), I thrashed. I ended up going to Scout Swimmer School in Coronado first, which was a two-week course, and a couple months later I went to Scout Sniper School. I checked into Scout Sniper School on October 2, 2003, and I graduated December 19, 2003. Our battalion had already left Camp Pendleton to do a UDP in Okinawa, so the five of us who just graduated STA had to fly to Okinawa to meet up with the rest of the battalion. While we were in Okinawa, we trained in various things while we waited for something to come up in the Pacific theater. Being in Okinawa, we are the early responders.

While there, Sonny went out drinking one night just to go out with the guys and have some fun. Well, fun turned into libo (slang for liberty, or leave) restriction for Sonny, and he lost his HOGs tooth. (A HOGs tooth is what you get when you graduate from sniper school. It's not a real tooth; it's a 762 bullet that hangs from 550 cord, an all-purpose cord used for tying shoelaces, rigging, etc.) "We were all drinking, and I went home with some Navy Corpsman chick. Nothing happened, which was weird [he grinned but widened his eyes to make sure I believed him, which I did], but I woke up late and missed a shoot we had that morning on the range. My platoon sergeant and platoon commander wanted to NJP [NJP stands for nonjudicial punishment in the U.S. Armed Forces] me, but I was in good with the company commander, because he was my company commander when I was in Alpha Company during the invasion earlier [when Sonny was in Fallujah], and he wouldn't let them NJP me. And then, sure enough, we were heading back to Iraq; I didn't even finish the UDP."

BACK TO FALLUJAH: 2004

In March of '04, one year later, I'm back in Fallujah, this time as a Scout Sniper. Our camp was named Abu Ghraib [Abu Ghraib was a forward operating base (FOB)], not to be confused with the prison Abu Ghraib. We did a changeover with the Army's 1/504th. Their scout platoon was garbage. I'm not trying to rag on the Army, but their scout platoon was garbage; they hardly left the wire. They would do satellite patrols around the camp, and that's it; they didn't push out. They could have done a lot more for interdiction and border interdiction; IED and rocket attacks were common. On our first mission there we walked out and walked back, from Camp Abu Ghraib to Route Michigan. Route Michigan cut Fallujah in half; it ran east to west. That was my, our, first time pushing out in enemy territory as a four-man sniper team. Our senior leadership was letting us get our feet wet. Everyone on my team had previous combat experience. Three out of the four of us went to school together; we were tight. This was at the time when the four guys from Blackwater got killed and strung up. We heard about it and then got the word we were going into Fallujah.

On March 31, 2004, four shocking casualties made news reports worldwide. In Fallujah, at that time, private U.S. contractors were being used to provide security in Iraq. This particular well-known and highly publicized incident happened in the city of Fallujah, involving four Blackwater contractors who were providing a security escort for a convoy of ESS trucks; a food-catering company that was going to pick up kitchen equipment from the 82nd Airborne somewhere in Fallujah. Reports state that the four contractors had never worked as a team before and were short two additional security guards when they set out in their two SUVs to escort the ESS trucks. Iraqi insurgents ambushed their vehicles. A crowd of anti-American protesters gathered nearby and pulled the four bodies from the burning vehicles out on the street and began to mutilate them. Afterward, they hung two of the charred bodies up on a bridge over the Euphrates River to parade as war trophies (http://www.pbs.org/wgbh/

pages/frontline/shows/warriors/contractors/highrisk.html, http://www
.cnn.com/2004/WORLD/meast/04/05/iraq.main/index.html). A few days
earlier, Iraqi insurgents had killed five soldiers near Habbaniya. With
these two heinous acts, the Marine Corps were ordered to mount a full
offensive retaliation assault on the city of Fallujah to eradicate the extremist elements (anti-Iraqi forces and foreign fighters). This offensive
was called Operation Vigilant Resolve. According to Global Security,
Scout Snipers were the core element of the strategy behind Operation
Vigilant Resolve. They were said to have averaged thirty-one kills apiece
during Operation Vigilant Resolve; one kill every three to four hours
(http://www.globalsecurity.org/military/ops/oif-vigilant-resolve.htm).

> The morning we got the order we were going into Fallujah, Bravo Com-
> pany 1/5 went to the southeast quadrant of the city, so our sniper team did
> the recon up to this soda factory there and set up an infrared trail guide
> (ITG), so when our forces came in behind us, they could follow the infra-
> red path we set up. To my knowledge, the soda factory wound up being
> a headquarters/staging point for us. This was the first objective for Bravo
> Company. The ITG is directional, so only the guys walking towards it can
> see the lights. You can't see them from the city even if you had NVGs
> [night vision goggles], if set up properly. So these lights would guide the
> rest of the company in once they figured out we were gonna make the
> breach to the soda factory. That night the company advanced towards the
> factory and fired two shots with the SMAW (83mm shoulder mounted)
> and makes a breach in the cement wall. Here we go! Well, the hole was
> for shit. It was about four-by-four-foot hole and two feet off the ground.
> People were carrying their three-day packs; it was a goat rope. We looked
> stupid all trying to go through this hole, but we went through it as fast as
> we could; you have to find humor in the small things for PMA (positive
> mental attitude). PMA is a sniper thing. Now everyone is running into
> the soda factory and clearing buildings. We almost had a blue on blue.
> [Blue on blue means they almost took friendly fire; fire from other U.S.
> Marines.] We had just cleared a building and were coming out behind the
> main infantry platoon, I think it was the 3rd Platoon, and they start laying
> down fire at us! It was quick and wasn't heavy. Everyone starts yelling
> cease fire and popping red star clusters. They were like twenty or thirty
> yards away. The pucker factor went up. They ceased fire, and we took
> cover up high on top of the building. We are covering their movements,
> watching our guys clear doors, and we have comms with them the entire

time as they are clearing; we are looking at dudes through the scope as we are talking to them, watching them, and covering down on them. It went down without a hitch and we took over the soda factory. We spent the night there with no issues. It wasn't until we got up to Route Michigan the next morning when things started to pick up in Fallujah.

Sonny's four-man Scout Sniper team was still together (to protect their identities, Sonny refers to them as letters). The team leader was "OR"; Sonny was the assistant team leader; "TG" was Sonny's spotter/ team SAW (squad automatic weapon); and "NK" the point man.

NK and I came up through the Marines together; we did our first deployment together, we indoc'd together, and we went through Scout Sniper School together. Shit starts cooking off on Route Michigan to the north, and we start engaging people while looking through the scope of the bolt gun. There are infantry on the road, infantry and machine gunners on the rooftop, and my team got up on a storage shed that was on top of the roof. Some of the guys had M40A1s, I had an M40A3, which at the time was the new thing. We didn't have suppressors, our scopes were still fixed (Unertl), and they weren't variable (Schmidt Bender). We were on top of the roof, we had machine gunners down to the right of us and infantrymen below us on the road; squads and teams were lining the road facing north on Route Michigan. We were facing north and we start seeing muj (slang for mujahideen) wearing the head garb and in full black dress, with RPGs and AK-47s, running across the road. The first time I shot someone, it wasn't even a rush, honest to God. In fact I remember the first guy I shot at, I missed! He was about five hundred yards away, we were on the rooftop, sitting supported, with our three-day packs in front of us, sitting Indian style with our guns' bipods on our packs in front of us. So we see this fat guy on the phone that my spotter is calling out. It's April '04; the ROEs were in our favor, kinda, for once. Pretty much you engage anything that has the slightest indication of being a threat. This guy was on the phone, it met our ROE, so I shot. My DOPE was good, and nothing! [DOPE is an acronym that stands for Data On Previous Engagement: information that has been entered in a log by a sniper that includes details of particular shots, such as rifle and ammunition performance, temperature, wind speed, altitude, etc. If the same conditions exists again, the sniper can use the recorded data to assist him in making an accurate shot.] The guy is still talking on his phone. I was like "what the fuck?" Apparently the bullet hit a telephone wire or something hanging in the streets about two hundred or three hundred yards out. The spotter actually saw it through the spotting scope. I had to redeem myself after that, ya know? OR and NK were facing north, and TG and I were facing west. There was an ICDC (Iraq Civil Defense Corps) compound a few hundred yards away, and past that a hospital; I knew because I could see the crescent moon on top. We started seeing muj in black masks appearing. TG was on the spot scope. Approximately 960 yards out was a muj. I could barely see him. I added the proper DOPE, and my first two shots hit a pole! I shoot again, and again, nothing! Where were the bullets going? We heard a "ding." So we are looking for poles, I'm looking through my crosshairs, the guys are trying to look where the bullet went, we see nothing. So I shoot again. "Ding!" I was like "fuck!" What am I shooting? Finally, I hit him with my fourth shot. I kept hitting a damn pole. I was lucky on the fourth one. Fourth time is a charm? I'm thinking I'm trying to shoot this motherfucker and I keep shooting a pole! This assclown is going to get away because I am apparently too eager to go to work, and I wasn't even looking for obstacles in the projectiles path. You have to find humor in it at the time. If you don't, you'll think you are the world's worst shooter, and that isn't good for morale. Maybe that's why my first kill wasn't a rush? What can I say . . . We were fortunate he was so far away that he didn't locate our position. He would have been in a world of hurt if they decided to come our way anyway. We had 11s (grunts/ infantrymen) and 31s all below us eager to get in on the action that was playing out in front of us. We had the upper hand.

THE IMPOSSIBLE SHOT TURNED INTO THE FORTUNATE MISS

Sonny and TG got off the roof and pushed into the city to Route Violet with OR and NK.

Our teams then split up. OR was the team leader and I was the assistant team leader, so OR and NK went with one reinforced platoon and TG and I went with another. I wouldn't see them again until I got back to camp after the Corps pussed out and pulled out of Fallujah. [When Sonny said "pussed" out, he was referencing his opinion regarding the politics of the time.] Lieutenant Palmer and Staff Sergeant Harrell had both been killed. One particular night, we were setting up in a nine- or ten-story building.

From this building Route Michigan was to our north and Route Violet to our west; we were facing west. Infantry and other Marines were to the south and east. We set up our stuff on the roof. We put an IR panel [an infrared signal to notify friendly forces of their location] up because the first night we got up there, one of our pilots (FAC) [FAC stands for forward air control] was calling in C130 gunship fire, and they were pounding shit all night. It was the coolest thing I've seen. Martial law was in effect so from either six to six or eight to eight; no one was allowed outside, especially if you were a MAM (military aged male). I was never the glory hound when it came to shooting; I never took the "head shot." I shot center mass, because you have the biggest margin for error. It was in this building, however, that I had a miss that I'll never forget, and I'm actually proud that I missed. So this old guy comes out of a building, and we ranged him at 650 yards out, and he's walking about three miles per hour, left to right, with this bag of rice on top of his left shoulder. So half of the bag is hanging out in front of his head, and half is hanging out in the back of his head. It had come over the net (comms) that the enemy had been transferring weapons in bags of rice. So there I was, twenty-two years old, ROEs being what they were, and I thought, I'm not waiting for authorization (which wasn't always the case back then, but we were trusted to make calls like this if the opportunity presented itself to make the call). This guy has a bag of rice, he's an enemy, and he must be transporting weapons. So I'm thinking, "He's a bad guy, and I'm gonna kill him." The platoon sergeant was there and he agreed with my call, so it wasn't like I was just acting on my own free will. It was a standing/supported shot. I adjust my scope and aimed center mass, like I always do. I can't follow vapor trail through the scope, but if you had a spotting scope for this it would have been awesome. So I get as comfy and calm as one can for a standing/supported shot (another reason why this story was ridiculous, because the only position more difficult to shoot from is standing/unsupported). There are men that probably rock both of these positions. I am not one of those men! Haha. So I get my breathing right, ease the trigger to the rear, and there's the recoil. All of a sudden the bag behind his head appears to, literally, explode in this cloud of white powder. You guessed it; it was a cloud of rice! Number one, that shit blew up behind his head, which would have been gnarly if there had been weapons in the bag; however, there were no guns in the bag. And the old man never misses a stride. He looks to his right, towards our position. He didn't know where we were, and if he did, he wouldn't have been able to see us. And then just shakes his head in disgust; that's what it looked like, anyway. Number two, it could have been a head shot from a standing/supported position from like 650 yards; it was close. Something cool to talk about with the guys whenever we swapped stories. We didn't kill him, and I thought, "Oh my God, I almost just killed an innocent person. I don't need a guilty conscience." I'll never forget that incident, because he wasn't a bad guy. That will probably stick with me forever; in a good way. That was the only time, up until that point and after, that I shot at a person, meeting ROE criteria, where I didn't know 100 percent if he was a bad guy. We were shooting on the probability he had weapons in the rice bag. [Sonny smiled and let out a sigh of relief as he told me the end to this story.]

TWO CONFIRMED AND DESERVED KILLS

Two days after the rice bag incident, Sonny and his spotter, TG, had attached to a platoon from Bravo Company and were pushing further into the city of Fallujah.

We had machine gunners (31s) with us; they weren't cleared to take shots, for whatever reason, but we were. We had just a little bit more training on target selection, and we had our optics to magnify the target. Oh . . . and we're not quite as crazy as machine gunners!! Love those guys. One afternoon, we had a report of a man and a kid with an RPK. The machine gunners get on the radio: "We got a man and a kid with an RPK, and we need a sniper." So we go to check them out. They were no more than one hundred yards away, but they didn't know where we were at, because we hadn't engaged any of the enemy from our location, yet. I shot the kid first; he had the gun. He was about twelve years old, I speculate. He met ROE, so I shot him. At twelve years old he can fire that RPK and kill us. The kid fell to the ground with the RPK. The 31s we were attached to watched the scene after I shot him and saw the older guy throw something over the RPK, trying to get it from the dead kid. He ends up getting the gun and runs around the building on the back side to the other side and is running down the alley about fifty yards away. A guy in our building, to the left of us, got on comms and said he had eyes on a man with a machine gun. The man had retrieved the gun from the boy that was with him and went around the building where he was and started to look for us, I assume to engage us. He was oblivious to our position because I shot him too.

Sonny ended up having to leave the "front lines" and return to Camp Abu Ghraib because of an injury he sustained. He was helping machine gunners build a machine gun position and was stacking sandbags. As he was packing one of the sandbags to into place, his hand slipped on the bag and into a broken window frame. There was a shard of glass sticking out of his hand, and Sonny ended up punching this shard with his right hand, which tore up his right trigger finger and middle finger. So he had to get back to Camp Abu Ghraib to get it taken care of. When he arrived at the camp, it was a ghost town. No one was there except a few guys who got injured. Their hooches (living quarters) were outside, and apparently while he was gone, two hooches down from his became the victim of a missile attack. The enemy was shooting 107mm rockets and shredded them. Sonny's hooch took shrapnel. "I saw the hooch and thought, I'm glad I was in Fallujah and not in the camp." (Which is a bit ironic.) The rest of his team were out doing IED and mortar interdiction. Basically, they were still out doing missions while he was stuck at camp with his hand in a cast. "It was tough knowing that the guys you have spent the last year with were still pushing out, a man short, and doing the damn thing." All the missions they completed that month went off without a hitch, and he was able to join up with the team a month later. By then their missions were sparse, and they had begun doing turnover with the men in 3rd Battalion/1st Marines (3/1). That wrapped up his second deployment to Fallujah. They got back stateside July 15, 2004.

In Fallujah, 2004, there was a bounty on snipers' heads. They pulled us out early before we could clear the entire city. Our platoon got a couple hundred kills. The other STA Platoon from Second Battalion/First Marines (2/1) did incredible work as well. Some of the best men I've had the pleasure of serving with came from 1/5. I still keep in touch with a lot of guys. A few are still in doing God's work, but most are out.

TRAIN LIKE YOU FIGHT

My parting words for anyone who wants to be a sniper, or who is currently; always train like you fight. Pack that extra two-quart canteen, that extra battery, extra ammo, because you're going be doing it anyway once you're in that situation, and it's better to have and not need than to need and not have. Two is one and one is none! Most of the guys do not come straight into a sniper platoon. Most have come up through the infantry, have a combat tour, then indoc and get accepted into a sniper platoon. You have to know your physical and mental capacity; know yourself (strengths and weaknesses) and be honest about it. Live meal to meal, day to day. You always take care of your boys, doesn't matter what you are doing, and take care of people in supporting billets, because in the end they are going to wind up taking care of you too. Treating people like dog shit, yelling at them, won't instill anything in them. Be a father and big brother. In that community, operating in a four-man team, you have to be tight. You have to trust the guy behind you is going to be on his game, which goes back to training. When you are training, don't just train to meet the standard; you have to train to exceed the standard. Are you giving 100 percent? Only you can quit, nobody can quit for you. Quitting for yourself is the same as quitting for your brothers. In a team you don't want to be the weakest link, because that will follow you. In our small community in the Marine Corps, your reputation gets around; it precedes you. And lastly, things don't get easy in a firefight. Quick decisions, snap judgment calls, maintaining comms, it's controlled chaos at its finest. Try not to get the "God complex" because of the position you are in and the life-altering decisions you have to make. Don't let it go to your head. Don't lose control and execute on the "T of two." Keep the faith and do God's work.

4

IT'S NOT ABOUT KILLING, IT'S ABOUT LIVING, AND SOMEHOW I LIVED

When I conducted this interview with Marine Corps Scout Sniper Timothy La Sage, I couldn't help but wonder when he would get his own movie deal. The story you are about to read will make you think about life, fate, and luck; it will make you wonder how he's alive today to tell it.

Tim grew up in Sussex and Germantown, Wisconsin. He considered himself to be a good kid; he learned discipline at a young age from wrestling as a sport. He went to church on Sundays and had a Christian education that he felt positively shaped his morals and manners. He was polite and opened doors for people and said "Sir" and "Ma'am"; he was raised well. He also fit the stereotyped image of a young, aspiring sniper. He had quite a unique opportunity to "rough it" when his age hadn't even hit double digits. His father, who was never in the military, was on a climbing team and went on rock-climbing expeditions around the U.S. He would take Tim and his older brother Peter along on the climbing trips. They would pile into his old Datsun pickup truck and trek across the country to the Rocky Mountains, Grand Tetons, or wherever, where Tim, who was eight years old at the time, would have to hike with his father, and his own pack, up to base camps (they were typically about five miles away). They, along with the other climbers, would set up camp overnight, so the next day his dad could climb while Tim and his brother waited for his return. There was no electricity, and while his dad scaled rock cliffs with his team, Tim and his brother were left to fend for themselves.

His brother was two years older than Tim and ended up joining the Army later on, when he was in his late teens. At the age of sixteen Tim got lured into joining the Marine Corps by a recruiter because he could get in through an early acceptance program. So at seventeen years old, he was attending Marine Corps boot camp. He was eager, in good physical shape, and he also knew his way around rifles, shotguns, and pistols. As a kid he would hunt on the five hundred acres of land that his family owned. He went through a hunter's safety course at the age of ten. He had never committed a crime, so he had a clean record. He could have been the Marine Corps recruiting poster child. (You will see as you read his story, that's kind of what he is.) Upon successfully finishing boot camp, he signed up for Marine Corps Security Forces, and then after his first tour there, he would go back to the infantry.

While in Security Forces, Tim attended Basic Security Guard School, which doesn't sound too challenging, or sexy. But as a Marine Corps Security Force team member, "you are not a mall cop; you need to have a security clearance so you can guard things like nuclear weapons." After graduating Security Forces, he was recruited for Fleet Antiterrorism Security Team (FAST) Company in 1993. Tim catapulted through his career in the Marine Corps, as you will see, from having a good base in mental and physical abilities as well as his expertise in handling weapons. FAST Company was one of the only special operations offensive units in the Marine Corps at the time, since they fell under the control of a Navy admiral. FAST Company Marines could deploy with Special Operations Command (SOCOM) elements due to their special operations training. Marines in FAST Company got jump qualified, certified as Scout Snipers and in close quarters battle (CQB) (how to clear buildings and neutralize any threats), and skilled in reconnaissance and surveillance. Because Tim's shooting scores were top-notch and he excelled at his physical fitness tests, he passed the indoc (short for indoctrination) into FAST Company without a struggle. While in FAST Company, he qualified with the Heckler & Koch MP5 9mm submachine gun (a weapon that is unique to FAST Company).

FAST Company was definitely operational. The primary role of FAST Company is to recover embassies that have been taken over. Nothing was really going on after 1993 and Somalia; it was kind of quiet until about 1997–98 outside of deployments to Haiti. During this time we remained active by deploying to England, doing exchanges with the Royal Army and Marines (training in urban conflicts due to their missions against the IRA and other terrorist organizations), training in mountain warfare to include high-angle shooting as well as tracking courses along with surveillance and deploying stateside. Some people raised their eyebrows and asked me, how can you deploy within the U.S.? Well, we did. We guarded nuclear subs when they were refueling or when they were dry-docked and provided security in high-threat areas such as around nuclear reactors, etc. It was an intense unit. Back in the early '90s we had the high-tech pager for that time. I remember being stationed out of Norfolk, Virginia, and we would be out at Hammerheads (one of the local dive bars that attracts a twentysomething crowd) in Virginia Beach at the oceanfront. Our beepers would go off, and we'd get called back to the command. It was our version of high speed. [He laughs and so do I, because I can picture him feeling "high speed" with his pager back then.] FAST Company was a great beginning to my career because it got me into advanced schools and training and a little bit of experience with real-world assignments providing security.

He also got to work hand in hand with the U.S. Navy SEAL (Sea, Air, Land) teams and Army Special Forces. After three years with FAST he changed commands. He left FAST in 1996 and moved over to 2nd Battalion, 4th Marines (2/4). While with 2/4 he deployed to Okinawa, Japan, and Australia for a Unit Deployment Program (UDP) where he trained constantly and honed his infantry skills. Upon returning from Okinawa, he went on postdeployment leave. To pass the time, he tried out for the Marine Corps soccer team, and he made it. He played soccer every day and met his wife, of seventeen years now, at the soccer field. He had to convince her that he was a Marine, because all she saw was this guy who would arrive at the soccer field every day around noon, who was never in a uniform and never carried a weapon, who was never training or shooting, so she didn't believe it when he told her he was a Marine. All he did, she thought, was play soccer, so she thought that if he was a Marine, he sure had it rough. He explained that when Marines come back from a deployment overseas, they usually get the first month off

as leave. During the next six months they could be put into the Fleet
Assistance Program (FAP), where they could get a job on base, such as
at the gym or with the Military Police, maintenance, etc. Infantry guys
would be lent out to other units that needed help. After that they went
back to their command again to begin training for the next deployment.

Playing soccer every day was great, but Tim would get bored with
that quickly. To his surprise, he was asked to come up to the 1st Marine Division Schools for his next assignment. "In the Marine Corps
you have three active-duty divisions, and in those divisions you have a
Schoolhouse that can teach and instruct units on a formal level. There
are many schools that can be taught there; however, the normal schools
are Scout Sniper Basic Course, MOUT—Military Operations in Urban
Terrain, HRST—Helicopter Rope Suspension Training, and Mortar
and Machine Gun Leaders Courses. Currently, you will also find Reconnaissance Schools under the Schoolhouse as well." He was a corporal at
the time, one of the very few corporals in the Marine Corps who was
not only allowed to, but asked to, teach other Marines, local law enforcement SWAT (Special Weapons and Tactics) teams, and personnel from
federal agencies, in urban tactics and CQB. Carefree soccer days in the
California sun were over. In 1998 he and his wife moved across country
to Camp Lejeune, North Carolina, so he could be an instructor at SOI
training Marines who had just graduated from boot camp. He was a
student in that very same classroom not that long ago. He warned his
wife, who was eight months pregnant with their first child at the time,
that their lives would need to adjust slightly, well, maybe significantly,
to his new job. Whereas back in California he had ample time to spend
with her, now he would be nonstop working and training; his life would
be much more regimented. She was completely on board, but it did take
a little more adjustment than she thought. Tim was always in the field,
and she was stuck raising their child. It wasn't fun with him being gone
over two weeks every month, but at least he still was in the country, he
would be home anytime he could be, and he wasn't out of sight or out
of communication, which she would soon experience in the future to a
challenging degree.

After two years in North Carolina with Tim running around chasing
and yelling at infantry students, focused on his career, and her running

the house and raising the family, she was ready for him to transition out of that unit. Tim admits she got the short end of the stick; "She was a young mom figuring out parenting, and she took that job on with no hesitation and gave it 100 percent, while I was working nonstop. I don't know how she did it. It was her show, her house, and I was a guest. I'd get hosed down outside sometimes before I was allowed inside. I usually spent my days yelling and screaming at students, and apparently one night she says I choked her out while we were sleeping, while yelling in my sleep for students to get into formation! We laugh about it now, but at the time she let me know that my behavior was, let's just say, not conducive to a family life. So I called my monitor up and told him to get me into the next deploying unit back at Camp Pendleton, just get me back over there in the infantry!" He soon left SOI, off to his next set of orders, which were to the next deploying unit out of Camp Pendleton. It was the year 2000 and he was back in California this time, attached to 2nd Battalion, 5th Marines (2/5). He checked in, and 2/5 already had a deployment coming up. "I asked the sergeant major, I was a FAST Company Marine, I'm a Scout Sniper, and instructor. Do you have any openings in the sniper platoon? He says, 'Awesome, you have a lot of leadership and Fox Company could use it; I hope you like the water.'" The CRRC (combat rubber reconnaissance crafts) would become Tim's second home. Even though it wasn't what he wanted at the time, that company ended up being a great time and experience for him. He trained in Coronado and was out on the ocean constantly, not a bad life. In a boat company in 2/5, he was always operational; he was on call for any piracy interdictions, water recovery operations, beach assaults on foreign soil, and any other joint task force opportunities.

In 2001, before 9/11, Tim went on another UDP with Fox Company back to Okinawa, Japan. While there, 9/11 happened, the towers fell, and within days they packed up their stuff, boarded a ship, and were launched as a reactionary MEU (Marine Expeditionary Unit) per se. Tim was on LSD-42 with Team 5 of the Navy SEALs doing antipiracy operations. "SEAL Team 5 was on our ship, and we did some joint operations with them. We responded to a kidnapping of an American husband and wife by the Abu Sayyaf in the Philippines. The husband was killed during the rescue attempt, but the wife was still alive. The

Philippine Army was tasked with recovery after the initial attempt. We had to move on to East Timor to assist the U.S. Support Group East Timor with humanitarian and civic assistance projects. Being in a boat company, we had the privilege to travel ashore, secure the hospital site we were assisting, and secure the area for the SEALs and the Admiral when they came to see our progress."

When Tim got back to the States, he got staffed out to augment the Military Police. After the 9/11 terrorist attack, all military bases were at heightened security and there were 100 percent ID checks and vehicle searches, so the infantry Marines helped man the gates. Tim went through a police academy to become an MP and therefore picked up his fourth MOS (Military Occupations Specialty). Tim was an infantry Marine, security force Marine, Scout Sniper, Close Quarters Battle Team member, formal instructor, and now a military policeman. "It was special to be able to go through a police academy because I was certified in law enforcement skills and specific training. I got to work with the FBI when the government started a joint database tracking system where we would track all the 'wrong turns' onto military bases all over the country. Along with being a road unit, I was able to apply my first responder abilities in highway accidents, domestic issues, and civilian unrest issues in the local community. Local police called us for support with immigration issues and deportation, and many instances of illegal narcotics citations issued to civilians who were searched when they accidentally came onto base."

Near the end of 2002, Tim got word that the Iraq invasion was getting ready to kick off. He was still in the FAP program, since the Military Police extended him because of his training. The problem was he wanted to deploy to Iraq; he wanted to be a part of this invasion and would stop at nothing in order to deploy. His temporary command, however, had other plans for him. They had just invested all this law enforcement training in him and he earned the MP MOS, so they wanted to keep him stateside. He knew there was no hope of them changing their minds, so one day after work, he just decided to check himself back into 2/5 on his own. They were eager to bring him back under their wing. There's a saying frequently voiced in the military, "It's easier to ask forgiveness than permission," and Tim adhered to it.

IN THE SECOND VEHICLE OF THE U.S. CONVOY INVADING BAGHDAD

Tim got back into his unit, 2/5, just in time. They were set to deploy to Iraq in two weeks. He was anxious, and somehow his wife supported his ambition. She was pregnant with their second child, Kenadie, and her husband was going off to war, not to man gates or patrol an ocean to thwart piracy, but to invade a country. It would be straight-up combat. He told me he feels bad now, but back then he spent those two weeks prior to going off to war at home watching war movies with the guys while prepping gear, sharpening knives, and getting into the mindset. (As he tells me this story, I think his wife must be a saint.) On February 2, 2003, he landed in Kuwait. Over 100,000 U.S. forces were berthed in "tent city" (what the military call a very large area of military tents). Tim and the guys in his platoon dug holes in the ground roughly three kilometers south of the Iraq border; that's where they berthed, once his company left the tents. At the time Mike Cerre, a reporter from ABC News *Nightline*, was following Tim's company. They adopted his unit to shadow throughout the invasion. Our nation saw war through the eyes of Tim's unit. While in tent city, Tim got word that an independent platoon was needed to detach from 2/5 and attach to 2nd Tank Battalion in order to protect the lead tanks from RPGs and small-arms fire while the tanks engaged in tank warfare. Although Tim didn't necessarily raise his hand and volunteer, he secretly and eagerly hoped that he would be assigned to this special mission, and he was. Tim and his platoon left 2/5 and joined 2nd Tank Battalion as a Division Reactionary Platoon. You may not know it, but 2nd Tank Battalion led the U.S. convoy in the invasion of Iraq as the lead of RCT 5 (Regimental Combat Team), and Tim's vehicle was the second in line.

On March 19, 2003, the president declared war on Iraq, and Tim's platoon got word that they were pushing to the border. On the evening of March 19, Tim's lieutenant said to him, "Sergeant La Sage, since we are the lead element, we just got asked to go on foot via compass and patrol in the desert up to this grid, and we have to leave in an hour." Tim and his platoon (the Division Reactionary Platoon with Fox Company 2/5) grabbed their rucksacks stuffed with everything they were living on and patrolled up to the border. Tim plotted the route and took point leading the platoon of forty guys. After digging holes for protection and waiting the next two days for the green light to cross the border, they finally jumped on AAVs (Assault Amphibious Vehicles) or "amtracks" for the invasion. The invasion was in four waves, or lines; the Army (3rd Army ID) led one line and the Marine Corps led the other three. Sometimes the roads were too narrow, so all four lines combined into one long line; Tim was in the second vehicle in that one long convoy of U.S. military vehicles. Think of a convoy that stretches from Washington, D.C., to Baltimore. There was one tank in front of him, all moving up to Baghdad. "You looked behind you and it was miles and miles of military vehicles; you look in front of you and there is one. It was surreal." Tim was really at *the tip of the spear*. According to the *Huffington Post*, 192,000 U.S. soldiers invaded Iraq that day (http://www.huffingtonpost .com/2008/04/07/a-timeline-of-iraq-war-tr_n_95534.html).

"The biggest complaint for recon (reconnaissance) and sniper units during that time was that units didn't stop long enough to forward deploy us properly, so we couldn't do our job. It was go, go, go all the time. I didn't have any complaints, though, because I was engaging the enemy on a daily basis for days on end without normally having to leave the amtrack."

While this convoy was making its way to Baghdad, there was no stopping; not to eat, sleep, go to the bathroom, or stretch their legs. The vehicles only stopped during those twenty-one days during the push to Baghdad to engage the enemy and refuel. There were anywhere from eighteen to twenty-five guys inside that amtrack with Tim, and more if they had to take prisoners of war (POWs) in the vehicle. "There's about four guys on each side of the vehicle on top, looking left and right. Everyone else is below, inside feeding you ammunition. It's packed. Since we only stopped basically to refuel, that meant we're in there for days. If you have to shit, you do it in an empty MRE (meal ready-to-eat) bag while you are shoulder to shoulder with the guy next to you." Tim laughs as he tells me, "You're stuck doing it on someone else's lap." I guess it is so gross and unbelievable you have to laugh. Once you do that, I can't imagine being too modest to do anything. "If you get sick, you vomit in anything you can find while someone's crotch is in your face. It's not pretty. And you don't sleep. You may try to, but the adrenaline pumping through you from being constantly fired upon won't let you. The ten-minute catnaps fueled the tiger."

Since there wasn't much space inside the amtrack, they could only bring as much ammunition with them as they could fit. All the chairs were ripped out, and the guys below sat on crates of ammunition. If they had to resupply, they had to wait until the convoy stopped so they could access the ammunition in other vehicles behind them. So when they engaged and killed the enemy, they would collect RPKs (Ruchnoy Pulemyot Kalashnikova, a Soviet-designed handheld machine gun), RPGs (rocket-propelled grenades, shoulder-fired antitank weapons), and AK-47s off the dead bodies killed in action and use their weapons as their "Recon by Fire" weapons. Recon by Fire was a wartime rule of engagement where they were able to engage dangerous areas without seeing the enemy. If they had to clear a room, they used their military-issued weapons for precise surgical firing. Sometimes Tim and his platoon would come across caches of weapons hidden in the ground and in staged pickup trucks loaded down with weapons, and they would collect them all or demo the cache.

As Tim was crossing the Iraq border in the second convoy vehicle, preparing to invade Baghdad and engage in combat on March 21, 2003, his wife, Jessica, was back in Camp Pendleton, California, giving birth to their daughter Kenadie. *People* magazine and the local Los Angeles news wanted to interview her because she had a "war baby," but she declined. Tim said, "She's not an extrovert by nature and didn't want to be bothered by the press and plastered all over the media. She just wanted to be with her healthy baby girls." Tim wouldn't even know about his second daughter's birth until three weeks later. Mike Cerre, the reporter for *Nightline*, came up to Tim, ripped off a little piece of notebook paper from his notebook, and handed it to him. On the paper it said, "6 pounds, 7 ounces, healthy"; that's it. That's all he knew about his daughter and his wife for another couple of months. He had no way to communicate with her; she had no idea where he was or even if he was alive. She assumed he was, because she knew the expected protocol, and the doorbell never rang with somber Marines in their service uniforms asking for Mrs. La Sage. I can't imagine just having a child, one of the happiest times for married couples, and you can't even talk to your husband until months later. There is no sharing in the joy and stress of the first weeks of this new life. And to add to the stress, you don't know if your husband will even come home after the war. If he doesn't, God forbid, he would never get to lay eyes on the life he help create that just came into the world. It's a sobering thought to those of us who don't have to go through that.

So while Jessica was with their newest newborn child, Tim was getting shot at continuously by the mujahideen and fedayeen Iraqi fighters. The shots were usually from combatants on either side of the road from the convoy who dug ditches and tried to fortify themselves or were hiding behind, on top of, or in buildings. The tanks in the convoy were shooting at enemy armored vehicles, while Tim's main mission was to keep the "klingons" off the tanks. (Klingons referred to the Iraqi combatants who would rush the tanks shooting and try to climb on top of them to grenade them.) The tanks were firing consistently. "If you've never been next to a tank when it fires, it blows your hair back even inside your helmet." Tim engaged in a lot of close firefights. When the vehicles did stop, it was Tim and his platoon's job to clear out all of the surrounding houses. He would jump out of the amtrack and run to the houses they were next to, sweep the inside, take the weapons, and take the POWs sometimes.

At one refueling stop the convoy started taking fire. Of course, they were sitting ducks, and Iraqis started shooting at them from about three hundred yards away.

One guy is on a roof and one is in the doorway of the house facing us. My partner Jay and I decide we'll each take one out simultaneously. As I squeeze off a round, I see this white flash, and I look up and see a white SUV coming to a screeching halt on the other side of the highway; I hit the SUV. And now the guy on the roof is really laying down fire. He's about 310 yards away behind a three-foot wall on the rooftop, and he's ducking down behind the wall after every time he shoots. The stress of being the only two firing back at the enemy, who's shooting directly at us, was deterred by Jay making fun of me for missing initially . . . which I made up for on my second press of the trigger. The enemy fighter was struck in the chest and folded down below the roof wall that blocked our visual. I could see it was a solid hit and he would pass; however, the thought of him being able to pop up and engage other Coalition Forces haunted me, since I couldn't confirm his death. This happened often, as we would engage the enemy while moving, and we couldn't stop. We would see the hits on our enemies, but it was so fast paced that you did not have time to verify or do "dead checks" most of the time.

MY WIFE GETS A VISIT FROM BENCHMADE

The convoy is still on its approach to Baghdad. On April 4, six days before entering Baghdad, they were passing the vicinity of Azizyah. Tim and his lead vehicles came in contact with heavy enemy fire. "This battle is later documented as the most significant battle against enemy conventional forces during this war." Tim was shooting at the enemy in a field from right to left.

I was shooting fast. As I hit the fifth guy, I took what it felt like was a sledgehammer to my ribs, and I fell down. I was expecting to see my guts hanging out. We are all wearing chemical suits at this time due to the Kurds being killed via chemical warfare the year prior, and we still had the unknown threat of chemical attacks. I'm trying to reach inside my gear to feel around my ribs and scoop up whatever I think is coming out, and I feel something moist, but nothing sticky. I realize it's just sweat, no blood. What the heck? I thought. I guess I'm ok. I looked at my flak jacket and it was ripped up on that side, and my body armor was odd, so I knew I was hit by something. Corporal J was next to me, and he was laying there; his face was jacked up, and he couldn't see through the blood. I cut his sling off his weapon and stood back up. As I stand up we take an RPG hit to the vehicle. I take shrapnel fragments to the head and face from the RPG hit. I fell back down again, and I see only LCpl K shooting out of the amtrack. He was doing the Rambo thing up there, going nuts on the enemy that were taking advantage of the lull in our fire. By now we had several Marines hit that have fallen into the overfull vehicle. One Marine, PFC C, was shot in the hand and oddly enough was laughing while doc was trying to wrap up what was left of his hand. Just about everyone that was outside the vehicle had been shot or took shrapnel. So I stand back up with a squad automatic weapon and grenade launcher and started working everyone out there; it was full-on mayhem. If you read a timeline history online, you will read that on April 4th Lieutenant Brian McPhilips was killed. He was the navigator for the tank element when he paid the ultimate sacrifice. We were supposed to go around Azizyah due to the known ambush waiting for us. When he got shot, we missed the turn and went straight into an ambush. It was rough. Picture a traffic jam and the first ten vehicles having to do a nineteen-point turn in a narrow street to get out of there and then drive back out of the city. It was pandemonium. I ran out of belt ammunition and grenades that day. I had shot all of the machine gun ammunition in that field, and then I had used all of the HEDP (high explosive/dual purpose grenades). I found out I was out of grenades to shoot when LCpl D's hand came up underneath me from inside the vehicle with my next round, and it's a green star cluster. One of the last enemy fighters during that episode popped out from a courtyard made of mud and grass. I ended up having to shoot at him with the green phosphorus. We all watched as the white circle that was at times closing off our consciousness due to heat, sleep and food deprivation was stalled by the green burn of the enemy fading away from us. It was memorable to say the least. Driving back out of that city and the firefight was surreal. I remember while we made our way back out and around that city it was almost peaceful as we drove. There was definitely time to reflect on those close calls as we CASEVAC'ed our wounded. The next firefight we had, we ended up losing our first sergeant, Ed "Horsehead" Smith. We knew before that we were not indestructible, but to lose First Sergeant Smith made us feel a bit vulnerable.

A few days after this firefight, we were stopped because vehicles were refueling, and I write this letter to Benchmade knives. How the mail system works is that you write a letter on anything you can find, cardboard box, wrappers, and you put it in an ammunition can and hand it off to the vehicles behind you and pray that it gets somewhere. So what happened earlier in that firefight when I felt the sledgehammer hit my ribs was that I got hit with an AK-47 round in the ribs, but it deflected off my Benchmade knife. The bullet penetrated the knife, but it boomeranged it enough due to its heavy construction to where it hit the side of my body armor. If that knife didn't deter the bullet's path, it would have penetrated my ribs and ricocheted around inside me against the inside of my body armor. God's will be done. I had a huge hematoma on my ribs with some lacerations. So I wrote Benchmade knives and tell them their knife saved my life. I had two knives in my hand before I deployed. My wife and I agreed that she would put one in her purse and I would take one to war. I took the Benchmade because it looked sturdy. Benchmade, like a Vietnam jungle boot, has steel on either side of the blade. I still have this knife with me today with a perfect hole through it. I sent this story in an ammunition can and who knows where it went or if it would ever get to Benchmade. Well, it apparently got there. Benchmade is located in Oregon, and when they received my letter their executives suited up, jumped on a plane, and flew to my house where my wife was. I'm still at war and still haven't spoken to her yet. They wanted to present me with a new knife engraved with my call sign, and she, having no idea of what happened, answers the door to see these men in suits with this knife they want to present to her now because her husband was shot! So she asks to read the letter I wrote, and mind you, I didn't hold back about what had happened to me, since it was to a business and not my family. She reads about my near-death experience in a firefight and the gore of war. Now, she's smart enough to know if I had been killed she would have been notified immediately, so she knew I was still alive, but in what condition? She had no idea. And I'm still in the fight while she's raising a toddler and a newborn by herself. I got a Purple Heart for that. I swore if I ever got hurt again, I would be the one on the phone with her going into surgery so she wouldn't have to hear it from a stranger first. I never have taken Jessica for granted, but I have definitely not made things easy for her. Having to have a stranger let her know if I was alive or not shouldn't be something she should have to go through. In fact, during a later deployment I called her one morning at 3 a.m. to tell her I was hurt very bad and was going into surgery to try save one or both of my legs. When she heard the phone at that hour, her heart must have stopped, but as soon as she heard my voice, she started to breathe again.

I told him she must be a strong woman to be able to deal with that. She doesn't have a choice, either. Tim agreed and even said he couldn't deal when his guys went on deployment without him: "I get this gross feeling." You have no communication with them but you are expected to be strong and go on with life just the same until they return, IF they return. That is a hard position to put people in, and yet it's done, with consent, all the time. No matter who is left behind "to keep the home fires burning," they have a very challenging responsibility.

Before the convoy neared Baghdad on the ninth of April, the four lines of the convoy split to cordon off the city. Some lines went northeast across the Diyala River toward Saddam's palace, some went to the Baghdad airport, and others went south to positions flanking the city. It was April 9, and Tim was sitting outside Saddam's palace under an overpass after completing a linkup with the Army's 3rd Infantry Division. They were watching jets do bombing runs from his amtrack. Tim doesn't remember to this day when or if he ever fully slept from March 21 to April 10. He was always up top in the amtrack and always awake. He took catnaps, but there was no sleeping. They finally got to exit the amtrack and enter Saddam's Almilyah palace, where possibly two American hostages were held. Before taking the city over, intelligence would report that Tim's platoon missed Saddam by only hours when the units were in the vicinity of the Iman Abu Hanifa Mosque.

I WORE THE MARINE CORPS FLAG LIKE A SUPERMAN CAPE

Tim was in Baghdad on the day our nation saw Saddam's statue being pulled down by U.S. forces. At this time 1st Battalion, 5th Marines (1/5) got themselves in a pickle. Tim and the forty guys with him in the Division Reactionary Platoon were launched to go help 1/5, who were caught in an enemy reinforcing ambush. Tim's platoon took three tanks and two amtracks, supporting 1/5, to go after the enemy. This was the first time in history since Hue City in Vietnam that the U.S. was engaged in urban tank warfare. They came upon a choke point where the enemy was reinforcing their ambush site against 1/5, there were three tanks in an alleyway with the lead tank shooting down the street at enemy technical reinforcing trucks, and the middle tank was stopped in a junction of other alleys with the rear tank in trace. "Iraqis are firing at them from tactical vehicles like something civilians have seen from Somalia. The main tank got stuck in an alleyway. It was banging its turret left to right and ends up knocking a light pole down, which lands on top. All the rubble from the surrounding buildings being hit with the tank turret, gunfire, RPGs, grenades, machine gun fire, and concussion from rockets being fired falls onto the tank and suffocates the turret mechanism. The tank was completely pinched and stuck. The second tank was about ten yards behind this tank and stops in the middle of a kill zone; there were a bunch of alleyways that met up, and that tank was pinned down by heavy RPG fire, and soon that tank is ineffective, since the street is too narrow to traverse the turret. We were engaging the enemy, so we instructed the tank crew to stay inside, since the volume of fire was impassable for them to get out. The third tank is stuck in last place, and it can't go anywhere or assist the others." So Tim and the guys went out on foot. They were in a huge firefight that lasted for eight hours, while on the other side of town the media was filming the celebration of the toppling of Saddam's statue. "People had no idea there was a full-scale battle going on, and I was in the middle of it. It was a crazy Hollywood scene. The enemy was trying to take the tanks, we were shooting at guys four stories above us, guys were throwing grenades at us that were going right across the bow of our tank into nearby yards, RPGs were hitting walls but didn't detonate, it was absolute mayhem for eight hours." Tim reached the guys in the downed tanks on the tank phone (there is a phone in the back of the tank to communicate to those inside) to see who was alive. "The guys in the tank were shaken up, the enemy were running amok outside; this was war! The guys in the tank told me they called in for air support. I can't talk to aircraft (high frequency vs. VHF) because we didn't have the same frequency in our ground-troop radios. So I asked the guys in the tank who they called, and they respond, 'Somebody, and we told them we had downed tanks and we need aircraft for support.' So I asked them, 'Did you tell them we were still here?' They replied, 'No. They said they are rolling in A-10s for support.'" Concerned and mildly frantic, Tim asked them, "Do you know what A10s are made for??" Tim explained to them that A-10s are designed to take out tanks. Tim hung up the phone and used the turret for protection from the enemy fire while still engaging enemy and avoiding the burning car that was twenty feet away. Through the entire invasion Tim had been carrying a Marine Corps flag inside his flak jacket and another corporal with him, Corporal J, had been carrying an American flag; they gave them to each other back in the States prior to going off to war. They both took out their flags. Tim proudly wore his like a Superman cape and Corporal J proudly waved his in the air because of what they thought was going to happen, which luckily didn't, while they were on the turret of a tank still shooting at the relentless fedayeen fighters and taking enemy heavy fire. Not more than two minutes after they had taken their flags out, leaning over the turret to see down the alleyway, shooting at people, the first A-10 came in, strafing right off their bow and into the alleyways.

All you hear is the glorious roll of the 30mm cannon on the A-10 rolling above you. He takes off in a high pitch and rolls out and everyone is in awe. Guys start laughing and cheering while still engaging the enemy that has now exposed themselves more to hide from the overhead fire. I start to laugh and yelled out in a pre-victorious bark, "DASH 2!" The second A-10 rips through the other side of us, raining casings on us. It was the whole nine yards, and wipes out a ton of dudes on either side of us. I would be remiss if I didn't recall the tank commander during this. At one point during this intense long battle I looked over at the lead tank and witnessed the officer out of his turret using a rifle over the alley wall at enemy fighters right to his side. Once he put the rifle down and drew his pistol we ran over to the front to support his firefight. It was quite intense, and the volume of enemy and gunfire was uncountable. War historians state that over one hundred fedayeen were killed during this ambush and our reinforcement attack. Two HMMWVs arrived behind our rear tank and passed us a tow bar for the middle tank, which was deadlined and immobile at this point. Jay and I hooked it up to the second tank. We still had fighting going on, so we had to ensure the team and others still have their machine guns down the alley introducing themselves to the enemy. We rigged the bar to another arriving rescue vehicle and had it towed it out of there. Once the vehicles were turned around, they drove off. The first tank I told you about is now able to reverse out of the alleyway; it flips a U-turn and drives off, without us! There's thirty-five of us, and all the tanks left us there. We had to bump through street by street doing the "Mogadishu Mile" (reference to when Delta Force and Rangers had to do the same after their battle). We made our way back to the Tigris River, where U.S. forces had a blocking position set up. While bumping and bounding (leap-frogging in general terms) across alleyways to get out, I remember looking ahead, and I could see a line of U.S. military vehicles. They are parked all next to each other at the end of this road up against the river. They're only blocks away; I can see people sitting on these vehicles eating and relaxing while I am still exchanging fire with the enemy. I'm wondering what the hell is going on? We finally get to the last building on the street and we are getting shot at by an enemy fighter. We shot an M203 grenade in the window so we could run to the front of the building that faced the river where all of our friendly forces were. We came around this building and we see this whole line, fifty-plus vehicles, armored, LAVs, all kinds of folks. Some of the Marines hanging out on top of them are yelling at us, "What are you shooting at?" Let's just say there was some cursing that went on, something to the effect of, "Hey assholes! On the back side of this building that you're eating lunch at, we're taking fire!" They had no idea, they were like wow, and they duck back down and put their helmets on. I looked around, and there were U.S. forces everywhere. Everyone was parked. It looked like the fight was over, like we just called "END EXERCISE" to a training event. It was highly weird. I remember I was sitting down on a log, I dropped my Kevlar, and I don't smoke, but this civilian guy sits down next to me and offers me a cigarette. I lit it up and burned it down to the end. I looked around, and the city was cheering. Cheering and looting, of course; however, the vibe in the air was of celebration. The civilian guy says to me, "You look like you just got done running a marathon." He looked as if they drove into the city and parked there eight hours ago for a nice visit. I was like, "How long have you been sitting here, what is going on?" He said, "Oh we are in the looting hours, it's pretty standard, you know, after the war is over, everyone just runs around looting. They've been doing it for hours now." So I tell him I just got done with an eight-hour firefight. He says, "Oh, that was you guys? We thought that was celebratory fire." Celebratory fire? Was he kidding? I basically told him to "F" off. Then he tells me he's a reporter for CNN and asks my name and if he can get a live audio feed from me to send back to the States. That was the first time my family heard from me; mind I couldn't talk to them, but it was the first time they heard my voice and knew I was alright.

Tim told me,

Even though you are in a firefight, you remember funny things that happened. At one point I'm leaning against the door of a house while shooting down the alley against several enemy in downtown Baghdad. The door opens and I half fall in and begin room-clearing mode. Well, there is a family in there that was supposed to be evacuated, and the dad has a gun. I don't shoot because he's not pointing it at us. Jay and I clear the room and disarm the man. They are all sitting there and one girl, who's in blue jeans, said, "I am Nadia. You need something you ask Nadia. Are you hungry?" We are looking at each other in disbelief. Nadia spoke English and went to Baghdad University. At this point, mind you, we've began eating chickens, or local food we have found since we were lucky if we received or rationed one MRE meal up front of the RCT. We are making fires in bookcases to cook chickens or making bread with what local houses had available. There was no food, no resupply, so what you find locally you ate. So we are in the middle of a firefight, I'm using their doorway as cover so I can shoot out of it, and she is in the kitchen cooking us macaroni, which we happily ate, in the middle of a gunfight! She would duck occasionally to avoid the bullets whizzing by through the house, but she kept on cooking. It was pretty funny then and now to us. I kept a log the best as I could during the war, and there were key words I would write, since we didn't have any time for full-fledged downtime. I remember wanting to remember the generosity of this family, so I annotated "Nadia" so I wouldn't forget.

MY ONE NIGHTMARE

At one point I'm in Saddam's palace, the next I'm in an alleyway in an ambush. During this particular ambush, picture three tanks as close as they can be stuck, and us just climbing all over them and around them, shooting at enemy. One of the houses nearby that we are trying to break into has this "Mozambique"-style shooter on top; he's lifting the rifle above his head and just firing anywhere, not even aiming. [I call it the Afghan style; if you watch the CNN documentary on the fight at Qala-i-jangi fortress at Mazar-e-Sharif on YouTube, you will see what I'm talking about.] We take down a wall with a grenade and jump over it. I'm taking point, blazing through this house doing CQB . . . there's a point to this story, but there has got to be a reason I was taking point that day, and I soon found out what it was. We were in a big room, we had four guys who were going to go right and a couple of guys were going to go left with me to clear this big thirty-by-thirty-foot room. The first thing I see going left is this guy in a muscle shirt, tucked into nice slacks with his arms straight out to his sides (insinuating a hands-up position, but they were out straight to his sides). There was another guy who was older, who sheepishly stood there next to him; he looked like his assistant. The guy in the muscle shirt definitely looked like an important person standing up straight and proud. It looked like he was an executive with his assistant. They are standing about ten feet away from me. I close the distance and I drop him to his knees without lethal force. Corporal E and D do the same with the other unknown in the room. We zip tie them both, finish clearing the room, then drag them outside. They are both standing there flex cuffed and amazed I didn't shoot them and wondering if I was going to now out in the street, as they would do to their own people. I point down the road and I kick the guy in the muscle shirt in his ass and sent him running. He stumbled a bit but then got his balance and took off in a full sprint. They both took off running. They weren't supposed to be there, and the city was supposed to be completely evacuated after notices were delivered of our arrival via our government to avoid civilian casualties. I go back in the house, and one of the corporals on the team is yelling for me to come to the back of the house where there was an alleyway. Well, there was an SUV parked there with the back end open. I walk over to the SUV and what do I see hanging there . . . an Iraqi general's uniform. There was a suitcase filled with dinar and another with U.S. one-hundred-dollar stacks and a third suitcase of clothes. It hit me; that guy was a general, and I just sent him running! I ran back through the house back to the street to see if I can see him. I caught a glimpse of him turning left about two hundred yards down the road, and there he went, out of sight. Evidently he was getting ready to leave town. To this day, that incident haunts me. It's the one nightmare I have repeatedly; he is the guy, my guy, who got away. He was one of the guys on the deck of cards. It is a gross feeling.

Tim didn't swear once to me while telling me this story, and he laughed a lot, but I thought he truly is a gentleman. If it were me telling this story, I would have been swearing like a sailor, but he used words like "gross." Now, that could be because he was trying to be on his best behavior . . . I don't know, but I bet his close friends reading this will. The deck of cards he mentioned were actual cards created by the U.S. military identifying the most high-ranking and most wanted members of Saddam's government. Tim then tells me for the record, "That was one time I didn't have to crap inside a vehicle because it was on his desk in his house—true story."

YOU CAN'T HESITATE WHEN IT'S GO TIME

"After Baghdad we moved up to Tikrit during Operation Tripoli looking for Saddam. We ended up in a battle in Ba'qubah uncovering large weapon caches. After several more months running foot patrols and hunting the enemy and establishing security in As Samarra and the Al-Qadisiyah district we returned to the States." During that war Tim received a Navy and Marine Corps Commendation Medal with Valor, a Combat Action Ribbon, and a Purple Heart Medal for wounds received by the enemy.

> With as many targets as we had, there were far more people (Iraqis) that surprised us who didn't shoot because they didn't have a weapon or there was women and children with them. We don't shoot unless we are being aimed or shot at. We never put ourselves in a position or our chain of command in a position where we had to explain anything . . . except for one time. That incident was televised and documented by ABC *Nightline* News. What ended up happening was I set up a choke point on a street, at "General's Corner," during one night when the vehicles were going to refuel just before we were going to go raid an Iraqi Republican Guard barracks, which was a Division Objective. About twenty Marines and I were going to take over the barracks that possibly had a large amount of enemy in there. We set up a choke point in a major intersection to stop incoming traffic. We moved a dump truck to protect us from any vehicles that wanted to race towards us. It was common practice: shoot a tracer round next to the incoming vehicle from the choke point, like a warning signal. We had a vehicle already attempt to run the checkpoint and after fatally engaging the vehicle, the driver was identified as an Iraqi Republican Guard general. Usually when the vehicles see the tracer, they stop. Up to this point, only enemy forces had tried to attack the checkpoints. It was simple stuff, and it works 99 percent of the time. This day we encountered the 1 percent when it didn't work. It's about 2 a.m. and I'm in the middle of my pre-combat checks and inspections getting ready to do the raid on the enemy compound. I'm probably about six hundred yards from the intersection where we had set up the choke point earlier, and I see vehicle headlights driving towards the choke point in the distance. I see the tracer round go off, then I see another tracer go off, and then a third tracer go off. All the while I hear the engine of the vehicle open up and accelerate. Then our machine guns open up in perfect angles of fire to stop the vehicle from running through the choke point, attacking, or being a suicide bomber. The vehicle ends up flipping over one of the ABC *Nightline* News reporters, Mike Cerre, and his teammate Mike, who is the cameraman; picture the General Lee in *The Dukes of Hazzard* sailing through the air, that's what this short bus did. Well, when the vehicle came crashing down to a deadly stop, the Marines went over to investigate, and they found that the occupants of the vehicle were all women and children, with one middle-aged male driver who apparently said screw it, I'm gunning it. Thankfully, ABC reported the grave news in a fair light of

the Marines because of the situations we were put in. That incident could have made the news with a different twist that would have projected U.S. forces in a really bad way. It was a horrid scene, and many Marines who heard the screams from the women and children that night, still hear them today. The Marines at that choke point manning the machine guns were nineteen-year-old, young Marines making decisions, the right decision; however, it's still a lot of responsibility for a nineteen-year-old.

I asked why the driver ran the gate, and Tim said,

Stupid is as stupid does. I have no idea. You shake your head wondering what goes through theirs. This wasn't a quick event; he was over eight hundred yards away from the choke point when the first tracer was shot. At eight hundred, six hundred, four hundred yards the vehicle was warned. At the very limit of an explosion ring we were forced to engage with the machine guns. He went from about forty miles per hour up to about sixty-five-plus miles per hour and gunned it towards the Marines. Stupid decision on his part, right decision on ours, and no ability to decide by his passengers. He was either heading to Baghdad or heading north, maybe trying to get women and children out? We have no idea. There is a reason why machine gunners and infantry Marines aren't taught to, nor expected to, hesitate concerning threats. Hesitation kills. Hesitation will breed delay, and the enemy will seize that moment. It's a horrible situation, on many sides; it looks bad for us, and then those Marines have to live with their decisions and what they did, even though it was the right thing. They have to live with the aftermath that the driver forced them to face.

I asked if there were any survivors, and Tim doesn't think there were, but he wasn't sure, because he heard the screams from the women and children from inside the van when he was patrolling to his raid on the compound. Even though they had a mission, I tell him I don't blame him for wanting to get off that target in an instant. He says, "Ya, that screaming stays with you." I can't imagine how the nineteen-year-old machine gunners felt that night, for doing their job. Tim told me what happened after was just as horrific. The young Marines had to pull all the bodies from the van and they buried them, thinking it was the right thing to do by giving them a proper burial. The next morning the unit made them dig up the bodies to turn them over to local authorities for a proper burial. So not only did they have to hear the screaming of the women and children as they were laying down fire on the van running the checkpoint, but they had to see the dead bodies of the women and children they just killed the night prior again, after being in the ground for the night. "That had to be the worst decision a command ever made, having the same guys who killed them dig them up. They should not see the humanity of their actions while still being asked to implement their skill set. They are professionals to the T, and to instill doubt is not conducive to preserving life."

PRIORITIES: I GOT TO DO MY THING, AND I'M GONNA DO IT AGAIN

It's the end of 2003, beginning of 2004, and Tim finally returned safely home and got to meet his daughter for the first time; she was seven months old. He told me that trying to integrate back into family life was interesting. His priority was to go off to war, and he got to do his thing; now his priority was to get to know his family, and maybe get out of the Marine Corps. "It was somewhat quiet in Iraq during the first few months until the beginning of 2004, when things start- ing ramping up again. 2/4 took over the Ramadi mission in Al Anbar province. They had a tough deployment as a battalion, and they were taking mass casualties." Tim says, "Perhaps it was because 2/4 was in Okinawa throughout the war and they weren't in combat. They never worked through their bugs like we all did in 2003. They got extended in Okinawa for six more months, so they were there for a year when the war finished up. They came back to the States and then deployed to the most dangerous city there was, Ramadi. 2/4 was getting a lot of enemy sniper activity." Back stateside, Tim took over the Scout Sniper platoon once Brent Clearman departed (RIP) and was asked to go assist and deploy again. He talked to his wife and told her he was going to stay on for one more deployment. He had about eleven more months at home before he had to head out again back to Iraq. He began training his guys in some unconventional ways. Being in FAST Company taught him a lot of skills he passed on to his team:

Urban sniping, urban patrolling, not just the rural stalks. For example, Camp Pendleton has a camp on it called Camp Talega. It's the farthest point north on Camp Pendleton where *Heartbreak Ridge* was filmed. Beyond Camp Talega is Orange County, California. There is a field, or valley, then a ridge lined with houses in Orange County. Up on this ridge was an animal shelter. So I'm trying to think of new ways to train my guys in urban warfare, and I have this idea about using the animal shelter. I ask the shelter if I can park a pickup truck up there to observe and spot my guys trying to sneak over to the shelter. I explained it was training, and I had spoken to the sheriff's department to clear it. They were fine with it. I sent my guys out on patrols, and they would have to do stalks to the objective, which was my pickup truck in the parking lot of the animal shelter. They were to get within two hundred yards of the objective and log in all activity in the vicinity. What I didn't tell the guys was that there were volunteers constantly outside walking dogs on and off paths and playing Frisbee—some obstacles to make their training a little harder. So they had to try different things to get around their scent being picked up by the dogs and not get compromised. I also trained them to move around malls and talk to each other without being next to each other. Being in mass personnel areas with a high flow of people would come into play during some street patrols or market area patrols later. We had lock-picking classes, etc. Other battalions started to get wind of how we were training, so 3/5 allowed us to train their entire sniper element with the help of their one Scout Sniper, which was about the size of their entire platoon at the time. I ran indocs and started screening guys for them so we could combine the sniper elements into one indoc—which hadn't happened in a long time. We trained them very well. BS and AD were crucial to this, as they were not going on the next deployment but were determined to have the best-trained platoon there could be. I was getting reports back as to what was happening with 2/4 in Iraq, and I was telling my battalion commander the techniques I would incorporate when over there. I wanted him to know we wouldn't just be sitting on our post; we would be unconventional. We would be more aggressive and proactive with locations we would use. The 2/4 sniper platoons were getting backfilled with infantry guys in country, since Scout Snipers are a limited resource (approximately 220 in the entire Marine Corps at that time). 2/4 had a Scout Sniper team with one sniper and 3 infantry Marines who were killed while on post. [You will read details about this tragic even in the next chapter.] After the team was killed, the enemy took the M40 sniper rifle off of the fallen Marine. We now have the enemy running around with one of our rifles, which will be used against us. It was our job, my job, to get it back and kill whoever took it. I failed in that mission but am proud as hell of 3/5 for not failing.

So, with his wife's consent, Tim is back in Iraq. Within the first week of being back in country, in Ramadi, the Weapons Company commander in charge of the area for Tim's platoon said it was too much for him, and he resigned his commission on the spot. This is highly unique and unheard of.

He's the unicorn; you never hear of that. Complete abandonment of his men. The battalion commander puts his assistant operations officer, French-born Captain Patrick Rapicault, in command, and within a week he gets killed. ABC *Nightline* again is following 2/5, and they chose to follow the Captain, who they had to tell the nation again of another lost Marine as they did for First Sergeant Edward Smith on the last deployment. I went to the battalion commander and said, "Sir, the chains have to come off." The enemy knows exactly what we can see from our positions, and we need to work around that. I told him what I would be doing and I would report to him the locations we would be working out of, and he said very well. It felt from that night on, we went out as Scout Snipers conducting mission after mission only to come back to refit with ammo and reequip. The enemy went from being confident with the upper hand to dumbfounded and confused at where to fear the eye in the sky they couldn't hide from. When we started incorporating our new TTPs [tactics, techniques, and procedures], I knew the enemy didn't have a clue as to what we were doing. We started engaging them from undisclosed locations, not where they figured we would be even if covered and concealed. They had no idea where we were. This was the time we were seeing "Wanted" posters up of us. Division Intelligence began reporting that the enemy communication began targeting us and putting out awards or bounties for Marines with scoped rifles. We had bounties on our heads, and we knew it meant we were doing well. It would also affect the snipers that deploy into the area after us, such as Chris Kyle and other SEALs who made the bounties on our heads public after our deployment in the area. We had to continue to get stealthier. We no longer did the typical HMMWV ride up to a building, enter en masse, and post watch up on the roof. The stuff we were doing went above and beyond. We were breaking into houses, picking locks, or quietly breaking locks. We were using all sorts of skills taught in Sniper School Basic Course and many others that were taught from a wide variety of expertise inside and out of the Marine Corps.

We would sit about seven blocks back from our objective with a visual tunnel on whatever we wanted to watch, then we would break into the house after watching it, tie up the entire family, and when we left we left them tied up! I don't care how they get out, but I am not letting them go so they could spread the word that we are in the area so we can get killed. And I'm not breaking any rules by keeping them tied; I'm just buying time and extending our lives. I could give a shit how they get out after we left, I'm not letting them go so they can rat on us and we get killed. More likely the next morning they got up and ran out. While we were in a house that we took over, we would make the women do their regular activities like making bread in the morning or whatever as to not draw attention to the fact we were in the house and shooting out of it. It was a target-rich environment. My goal was to make sure our battalion commander (Colonel N) didn't have to answer for any of our shots that we took.

TAKE THE REPORTER INSIDE THE BUILDING

One incident got a little too close for comfort that could have caused the Colonel concern. We had been in this house for a day and half, and I've already laid out the distances to the intersection outside, to the buildings nearby with dark shadows that I can't see into. I assessed the area and knew it pretty good. So as we're sitting on a roof looking down the road, we see this guy on a moped with a guy on the back circling the intersection I told you about. There was a hole in the ground in the middle of a roundabout in the intersection. Sure enough, "Moped Joe" comes around, circles the hole twice, drops the guy off on the back who has a pack, and then the guy tries to drop the bag in the hole, and then I drop the guy with the bag. The guy on the moped takes off. One of the other sniper teams in that building with me, "Shadow 4," takes a shot at the guy on the moped but doesn't get the hit, and he disappears down the alleyway and he's gone. About ten minutes later Moped Joe comes back again, with another passenger on the back, circles the hole, and drops this guy off near the hole. As he goes to drag the bag to the hole, because the bag is just lying there on the ground still, Shadow 4 drops him. This scenario goes on for another forty minutes with each of us taking turns at shooting. The COC (Command Operations Center, pronounced as *see-o-see*) and I talk via radio. The watch officer tells me I never have to call in for permission for anything; I just have to do my job and report it afterwards, which I already knew. I had called in the two previous kills, "Be advised Shadow 8 engaged, Shadow 4 engaged a guy on a moped dropping off passengers with a bag they are trying to conceal in a hole, etc." "Roger." Again, "Be advised moped guy is back, Shadow 8 engaged second passenger trying to put the bag in a hole." So then I call up and say, "Shadow 8 requesting permission to continue to engage targets from moped." The reply back was, "Shadow 8, you've never called in permission before, just stay up there and do your job. Are you alright? What's wrong?" I reply back, "Well, I just want absolute permission to engage these targets when the age group of his passengers has gone down in the last forty minutes from twenty-five-year-old males to now boys the age of my daughter (younger than twelve)." COC gives the "ceasefire" and said they would send in armored HMMWVs to try to deter the situation. So some of the mental aspects of what we do while deployed tie back to your home life. I know you have to give 100 percent attention to the mission, no matter what it is, to be successful. You have to compartmentalize. I would come back from the mission, send an email to the wife, once a week at best for ten minutes we would talk on the satellite phone, but that's it; other than that, it was 100 percent live, eat, breathe my weapon, my next insert point, and my extraction.

When you're sitting out there, and *American Sniper* covered it, you have some hefty decisions to make that weigh on your conscience. One time we were patrolling with a company of infantry Marines, about one hundred to two hundred guys. We were doing a sweep through the city and we end up taking machine gun fire, and we all scrambled into different buildings. My snipers and I, along with an Associated Press (AP) reporter, jump into a house. Shadow 4 and I are up on the rooftop. A couple guys are inside the house to make sure nobody bombarded it. It was a two-story house at the end of a long, T-shaped road. So we are at the "T" looking down this long road taking heavy machine gun fire from about four hundred yards down the road from both left and right sides lighting up our building. The reporter on the rooftop with us is lying in a fetal position, crying with his camera sideways, snapping pictures, saying, "I hate my job! I hate my job!" Meanwhile, the infantry Marines in other buildings were dealing with their own firefights from surrounding enemy. We were trying to punch holes in the brick wall so we could get a visual and try to engage the enemy. Then we start taking heavy fire on both sides of the building. We're all crouching down and running around as low as possible. Two other Marine snipers with us, Barrow and Hubbard of Shadow 4, are taking shots; they later were killed on another mission that deployment, God rest their souls. We try to put the .50-caliber SASR to work because we can see where they are shooting from but we can't see them. They are shooting from these hacienda-style courtyards and engaging us heavily. We are trying to shoot through the courtyard steel doors; no luck. About five to ten minutes into the firefight, one side of the street stops firing. We don't know what's going on. Then we see this little girl walk over from the quiet side to the active side. She goes in the building and comes back out minutes later with a belt of ammunition to resupply the quiet side! They send her over twice across the street to get more ammunition, and at some point we had to say, we have to stop the source of this problem. The team leader and myself know what needs to happen. The other guys are on their rifles. Who can live with that for the rest of their lives?

Tim had young daughters at home. If he did it, would he be reminded of it every time he looked at his little girl? This is what snipers have to live with. We all have tough decisions to make in life, but I don't think many can compare to the decision Tim and his team leader were faced with that day. So the enemy sent the girl over for the third time. Shadow 4 section leader and Tim were forced to make a decision.

That's why we get paid to make the big decisions. We're pinned down, we have an AP reporter with us, whether you shoot the girl or you don't shoot the girl, there is very bad story that is going to come out of this for the girl or for our families. Shadow 4 section leader and myself decided to have him take the AP reporter into the house. Then the machine guns were silent. Some of those decisions that your training has prepared you to make, still sit with you when they shouldn't, because you know it was the right decision, but they still never leave the mind. You know that the people you are fighting beside, and the people back home in my country want me to do this, and I understand the politics and agendas of people, but what people don't understand is what our (snipers') agenda is. People will tell us that it's to kill, but as a Christian kid who grew up with morals, my agenda was to stop the genocide, stop the people who are causing the genocide. If that means to stand up and take action, then so be it. When you look at Ramadi on Google Earth and zoom in, you can see that a third of the city is a graveyard/body dump. They would just dump the bodies of people who didn't want to conform. People who they shot in the head, women they raped, they threw them all in there. The bodies numbered thousands, so who would I be as a man not to take action against that and stop it? I have "engaged and neutralized" many targets, but I have kicked soccer balls around and shook hands with a thousand more Iraqis than those that I have neutralized. The ones I have killed are trying to kill us, and killing innocent people. People don't understand that. If someone wants to shoot at me, I'm going to shoot back and protect my life. Some say, but "you are in their country"; yes, but I'm trying to save the majority of that country's people from the genocide I can see happening in front of my own eyes. I have patrolled through that graveyard, ten guys walking at midnight through this ten- to fifteen-click [a click is a kilometer] graveyard to the south of Ramadi so we could watch the city from the darkness; that was haunting. And we'd catch locals sneaking out there at night! There's people in the USA illegally, but I don't go around shooting at them, like I shouldn't be shot at for just being in Iraq; does that make sense? Back home doesn't always understand this; they haven't seen or smelled the bodies, heard the screams, or understand the mass killings of the Kurds to the north. Ramadi was the wild, wild West. It was full-on engagement 100 percent of the time.

JARED HAD THE LAST LAUGH, GOD BLESS HIM AND HIS FAMILY

While inserting to do pre-raid surveillance on Abu Musab al-Zarqawi, I was crossing a dark alleyway over a median on an ambient lit street into another dark alleyway, making our way to a house. It was typical fashion for the two guys on point to peer out from the darkness to look at the length of the street in the direction we are going to move to, bound across the street (like leapfrogging), then the next two go, and so on. On this particular night, the first two Marines, Blake and Grimes, looked left and right, bounded about twenty yards across the street and into the next alley, facing forward. The next group of guys to go was Hubbard, Barrow, and myself. As we go across the street, someone detonates an IED daisy chain. This IED was meant to take out armored vehicles, and we were on foot. I sailed across the street from the blast and landed at the entrance to the next alleyway. I immediately get up and start scurrying over to the middle of the street to regroup on the safe side. I come across Shadow 4, Jeremiah Barrow, and he has a huge hole in his chest. He's gone. I can see Jared Hubbard laying in the street nearby motionless, and I run over and start stripping him down, checking his vitals and looking for wounds to no avail. Checking his groin and armpit for artery bleeding, I can't find any bleeding, so I start chest compressions. He had been dipping at the time he died, so I go to do mouth to mouth and get a mouthful of his dip. God bless him, I love him. I cleared his passageway and start doing chest compressions. Jared and Jeremiah were about two feet on either side of me, and they both died instantly from that IED; somehow I got launched about twenty feet. I had severe leg injuries and shrapnel everywhere, but somehow I lived. The two guys on point still in the alleyway both lived, but they each took about eight or ten holes in their backs, and one of the guys' arms was shattered and filleted. On the friendly side of the alley the next Marine to bump across holding security took facial shrapnel. We ended up dragging our two best friends off the street into a compound yard area. We are all in a circle around each other, performing first aid on everyone. While I was still trying to resuscitate Jared, another was putting tourniquets on my legs. I'm doing chest compressions with a pistol in my hand and Grimes is trying to get a radio functioning after being damaged. We're collecting weapons, because at that point I'm thinking one, we are going to get a counterattack, and two, we are still looking for a stolen Scout Sniper rifle that the enemy has and there are now more out in the street. We destroyed the stuff we couldn't carry and from there . . .

(At this point in the story Tim let out a sigh and stumbled for words. He's an upbeat guy, but I heard the anguish in his voice as he recalled this story. Even though it was a phone interview, I could hear when Tim smiled as he talked; he was not smiling now. What I heard created a mental picture of him contorting his face in disbelief, and he continued on.)

. . . it sucked a little because it took forty-five minutes . . . what ended up happening was, well the story is . . . since we got blown up, the raid force was to take down this particular house if anything happened to us, so they launched a medevac team with that raid force. We were inserting to do pre-raid surveillance for a high-value target, Abu Musab al-Zarqawi (mentioned in *American Sniper*). The eight of us waited about forty-five minutes, bleeding out, and finally two HMMWVs find us and we load up one HMMWV with the two dead Marines, the two pointmen that were wounded severely along with all the gear, and the remaining Marines besides myself and one other, since there wasn't any more room by any means. My pants were basically blown off, and I could fit a beer bottle through one of the holes in my leg. Another hole shredded my opposite calf. The one HMMWV drives away, so another Marine and I are waiting to get in the other HMMWV. Well, it drives up to us and then by us, following the first one! We are sitting there stranded. So I had to convince the homeowner of where we're at to give us his car by showing my pistol and a $20 (we kept money on us in case we had to bribe someone—for instances just like this), and I said, "car keys." He spoke English for the first time and gave me his car keys. All I could think was that some lance corporal on post is gonna wax me when I try to enter Hurricane Point— the battalion compound across from the 1st Marine Division camp ("Blue Diamond")—but I'm gonna give it a try anyway. I need to get us back to the base with west side of Ramadi. So I tape big "X's" on the hood of this Iraqi's car with duct tape, I put my IR beacon on the antenna, and I put IR ChemLights on the windshield wipers. So we borrowed his car and medevaced ourselves back toward camp until a link-up was made.

Tim made it back to camp, and he made it back home, as you will read.

PTSD IS NOT A DISORDER; IT'S JUST ANOTHER REALITY

As a sniper, you are given the trust and confidence and the ability to be judge, jury, and executioner. You have all these responsibilities and then you get hurt, and all that responsibility is over. I got hit by that IED on November 4th. I called my wife right away, like I had sworn to always do after that first time being wounded. I went through surgeries at Charlie Medical; a triage camp set up for the area, TQ (Al-Taqaddum), South and North Baghdad, and then off to Landstuhl, Germany. I was home at my house on November 9th. There was no Wounded Warrior Regiment in place back then. There wasn't appropriate accountability nor medical care coming back when you returned to the States unless you had a full amputation and were hospitalized (or should have been like I was but was not). I woke up at my house, which was on base, in my own bed. The last conscious memory I had was being in a hospital in Walter Reed. I had remained unconscious on all flights while the flight nurse administered morphine. I had zero hospital care for six months. So picture going from the battlefield in that chaotic environment and then you wake up home in your bed. My daughter, who was five years old at the time, was preparing gauze with saline solution for me, my wife was cleaning out and packing the rotting flesh wound I had in my leg three times a day. A volunteer fireman luckily helped us out, along with out-of-state family and also the newly started Injured Marine Semper Fi Fund. I lived on base in base housing. My wife would drive over to medical to pick up the supplies I needed. Week after week she told them I was still bleeding, and all they did was give her a grocery bag with more gauze, saline solution, and painkillers; they wouldn't come over to the house to check on me. There was no tracking, the hospital was full, I was like a ghost, and they didn't know who I was, when or where I got wounded, so "we" took care of me. After five months the smell of my rotting flesh consumed the house. I lost all the muscle in my leg as the adductor muscles rotted. As I sat there I thought, a minute ago I was king shit with all of this responsibly for the Marine Corps, and now I'm left immobilized with a rotting flesh wound and they won't even take care of me. I was forgotten. It happened to so many guys. Wounded Warrior Regiment is assigned to track down these guys, guys like me, and make sure they get the proper care they deserve. I was supposed to be admitted at Camp Pendleton Naval Hospital or Balboa in San Diego when they flew me sedated into Miramar, but I got lost.

Tim tells me he most likely has some PTSD (posttraumatic stress disorder). "I hate the term PTSD. It's not a 'disorder'; it's a reality, it's a different reality, a posttraumatic reality. Look what we go through and then we abruptly wake up back home and are expected to assimilate just fine. You know you would think after the World Wars, Korea, Vietnam, the government would have had a plan for the wounded guys when they come home from OEF and OIF. There's abandonment issues, anxiety issues, the VA hospitals are backlogged, etc. I ended up going to hospital in town after six months being home and got skin grafts and got taken care of. I spent eighteen months of living on base, no shaving, no haircuts, no working." He must have felt like he was losing his identity. "Then the Marine Corps tells me they are just going to medically retire me. Well, I want to stay in; I want to work. So then they started giving us wounded Marines the opportunity to stay in. I enjoy being a Marine first and foremost, I enjoy being a Scout Sniper. So many people ask me, 'What's your best shot?'" Tim was surprised when I never asked, nor cared to ask, what his best shot or furthest shot was. That is not the point of this book. He told me he's been asked before, though, like it was the most important thing about being a sniper, and he says,

I tell people my best shot is at twenty-five yards. At that point you'd damn well better have a tight plan on how you are going to defend your position, escape your position, and how you are going to kill everyone in the process, because people are coming at you, and you better be ready. At five hundred to a thousand-plus yards you are laying in prone, you are breathing, you're calm, it's peaceful, and you are applying your fundamentals. I tell people, it's not about killing, it's about living, actually. It's about watching our convoys go up and down the streets safely, it's about soldiers coming back and being able to sit with those guys at the chow hall because you just knocked off the dude that was going to slip an IED in a hole in the middle of a traffic circle; it's about the guys who live. It's not about being the crazies going into churches or schools shooting up a bunch of people, it's about being the guy who shoots these people before they conduct mass murders. I can break bread with my friends, with my brothers, and see a movie or attend a congregation and not have to worry about a crazy person to mow us down with gunfire because there's someone watching for him, there's someone in the hide waiting to eliminate him so the rest of us can go about living safely in peace.

5

YOU HAVE TO BE READY
TO BE UNCOMFORTABLE
TO BE SUCCESSFUL

"I don't want to talk about shooting people. Quite honestly, I'm not the gritty sniper dude. I was a sniper, I am proud of it, but I wasn't born to be one like some guys are. My buddy Tim [Timothy La Sage, whom you have already met in this book in the previous story] was born to be a sniper. I did well, but I wasn't perfect by any means. I was really all about taking care of my Marines." I tell Fritz, this isn't a gritty sniper book. In fact, I haven't asked any of the snipers I interviewed what their best or longest shot was or how many people they killed. He replies,

Ya, cause that doesn't matter. I'm not a "sniper-phile"; I don't masturbate to gun magazines. At the time I was a sniper, I cared more about my Marines and their safety and their effectiveness on the battlefield than . . . "there I was . . . looking down the scope." Anyone who talks like that probably didn't really do it, not really. I know how flashy the sniper community is to others. It's what attracted me to being a sniper when I was younger, and I'm glad I got to do it when I did. My experience as a sniper was unique in the fact that I was the platoon sergeant in a Scout Sniper platoon in charge of roughly twenty-five Marines, about half of which were snipers and the other half who hadn't gone to Sniper School yet. Before I even went to Scout Sniper School I was a squad leader as a corporal, and I had already been on deployment, so my path to becoming a sniper happened when I was a little bit more mature than what the

Marine Corps is usually looking for. But because I had good leadership who supported me and allowed me to leave my company, even though I was in a leadership position in the infantry, and because the stars just happened to align when the indoc came around (indoc for Scout Sniper School happens once or twice a year), I was able to get into the indoc, and I passed. I was just about to lead my squad on a deployment to Okinawa when the indoc came up. I had always wanted to be a sniper, so I thought, it's do or die. I asked if I could take the indoc, and my platoon and company commanders let me. If you pass indoc, then you can attend Scout Sniper School. Because I was so senior, *ha*, in relative terms, I was a nineteen-year-old corporal, I spent three weeks in the sniper platoon before going to Scout Sniper School, which is a rare event. In the Marine Corps you refer to the school-trained snipers as HOGs (Hunters of Gunmen), and everyone else in the platoon who hasn't gone through Scout Sniper School yet, as PIGs (Professionally Instructed Gunmen). Usually you spend six months to a year living as a PIG earning your way to Sniper School. I showed up to the platoon, and three weeks later they asked me if I was ready to go Sniper School. I didn't even know the definition of Marine Corps Scout Sniper. I had no idea what was going on. I was a good infantry Marine, but I had never put a ghillie suit on, I didn't understand two-man tactics, I was fresh out of the infantry. So my indoc was in Twentynine Palms, California, in the desert in late May. In seventy-two hours we covered over 100 miles in 100-degree heat with four hours of sleep. Each indoc is unique, so if you are in Camp Pendleton, you are in the mountains, if you're at Twentynine Palms you get the heat and the sand, if you're at Camp Lejeune you get the humidity and the bugs, and in Okinawa the humidity. I can't talk about the indoc specifically, but it was a very, very hard thing to get through, but I made it.

The motto in 1st Marine Division (1st MARDIV) Scout Sniper School in 1999, when Fritz went through, was "Suffer Patiently and Patiently Suffer." It's since changed, but this motto reverberated not only throughout his career as a sniper but his entire career in the Marine Corps and in his life.

After Scout Sniper School he PCS'd (an acronym and term used in the military when military personnel change assignments or stations and have to move; it stands for Permanent Change of Station) to the Pacific Northwest, where he was in a Marine Corps Security Forces

Company doing security guard work. He also was part of the CQB (close quarter battle) Team, similar tactics to law enforcement SWAT (special weapons and tactics) teams; he wasn't doing sniper work. Fritz was a twenty-six-year-old, newly promoted staff sergeant who had been married for about three years and just had his first child. In February 2004 his dreams came true; his orders changed, and the Marine Corps assigned him to a sniper platoon. He was going to get to do the two things he loved doing most in the Marine Corps: being a Scout Sniper and leading Marines, "the best of both worlds," as he calls it. That meant he, his wife, and their newborn child had to leave the serene "twilight territory" and trek down south to their new home in Camp Pendleton, California. Up until that point, Fritz had been at a nondeployable unit with the Security Company, which had its pros and cons. Because he couldn't deploy, he was able to stay close to home, just like a typical suburban dad who has a thirty-minute commute to work every day and who comes home to the family and dinner every night. He and his wife were able to build a strong, stable relationship, and he was able to be by her side when his son was born. It is common for wives of military members to have to go through childbirth alone, without their husbands, because they are deployed. Some military husbands don't even get to meet their child until they are months old. That's a hardship, unfortunately, that just comes with the job. Fritz knew he was lucky, but he also felt the pangs of remorse in a nondeployable unit. When 9/11 happened and the U.S. kicked off Operation Enduring Freedom in Afghanistan and then Operation Iraqi Freedom in Iraq, Fritz wouldn't be a part of either invasion; he, along with the rest of the infantry Marines in his company, would be staying stateside because of the job they were doing. So he felt like he was on the sidelines watching the wars. But he knew that his new unit assignment in California would change all that. He also knew it would be a total change of life for both him and his wife, who were very comfortable living as a married couple in the Pacific Northwest. But his wife understood how much this meant to Fritz, and just like he stood by her side during childbirth, she stood by him during his career in the Marine Corps. Unfortunately, she wouldn't be by his side, literally speaking. Fritz would soon be thousands of miles away in a hostile territory watching people get killed, writing a death letter, and hoping he wouldn't be one of those statistics. She would have to stay behind waiting for him, in an unfamiliar area, raising a child by herself, taking care of household business, worrying about whether or not her husband was alive and well, day in and day out, for months.

It was a cold, dreary day when they packed up their Subaru Outback (something you envision to be the quintessential car for those living in Pacific Northwest or somewhere with rough terrain and an adventurous landscape) with their five-week-old baby in the backseat. They got on Route 5, which extends all the way from the border of British Columbia to the border of Mexico, and drove south for about two thousand miles to Orange County, California, Fritz's new station, Camp Pendleton. After the two-day journey they pulled up to the front gate of Camp Pendleton around midnight, exhausted and blurry-eyed. He says he'll never forget that first night.

I have a vivid memory of my first night in California. There were a lot of things going on at that time; moving, driving, going back into the infantry, new baby . . . it was a lot. My "new" platoon was cross-training with a sister platoon, another platoon in the same regiment. They were all going on a run and wanted me to go along. They invited me so I could get a sense of what the platoons were training in, but I knew the invitation was really a test. I was their new platoon sergeant, and they wanted to know if I was going to go out on this death run after having just driven twenty hours, a majority of which was stuck in LA traffic, with my wife, whose nerves were fried from being in the chaos of California. Thankfully, we were blessed with the best baby ever; he never cried and was an angel on the ride, so he was what held it together for us. I had very professional snipers in this new platoon, and they took their job very seriously. Most of them were OIF 1 (Operation Iraqi Freedom, "1" refers to the initial invasion of Iraq) vets, so they were testing their new platoon sergeant, who just came from a nondeployable unit and had never been tested in combat before. It was around midnight or 1 a.m., and most of the Marines were sleeping. The few who were up came over to me and said, "We're taking them on a run. Would you like to join us?" That was the invitation. Of course I can't say "no," even though I was mentally exhausted from traveling. So I said in a chipper, enthusiastic voice, "Sure, where are we going?" The Marine replied, "To the beach." I thought, oh, cool, I can handle a run to the beach; after all, I am in California. It would be nice to see the beach after that drive today.

They woke the Marines up, and off they went on their beach run at 0100 hours. What Fritz didn't know was that the beach was about seven miles away, so this was no jog along the oceanfront; this was a half-marathon run to a beach that felt like quicksand, and back. It was a little bit of a surprise to him; thank God he had been drinking water on the drive that day. But he had just proved himself to his sniper platoon. "I think it was a good introduction to my new sniper platoon."

DEPLOYING WITH MY BROTHERHOOD

Sniper platoons are a brotherhood. I guess the camaraderie amongst us comes from the fact that we all have similar personalities in a way; we were all attracted to Scout Snipers, to that kind of job. Hollywood likes to typify the sniper character as someone who was raised in the sticks and grew up hunting, who is good in "field craft," and even though you need these skills, we all don't come from those backgrounds. I grew up in Southern California and Colorado riding BMXs and snowboarding. My parents were from Massachusetts; I call them "civilianized democrat liberals." I was definitely a different cut from the rest of my family. No one in my family was in the military, except my dad, but he was drafted in the Army and had a bad experience. On my seventeenth birthday I signed the dotted line and joined the Marine Corps; it was my birthday present. My dad vehemently opposed it. My parents were divorced at the time, and he told my mom he wouldn't stop me from joining, but that if I joined, he would stop paying the rent for the house we lived in; but if I went to college, he would continue to pay rent. My mom let me join anyway. My brother had just died a couple years prior, but I had to get out of the house. I was a free bird. I give my mom a lot of credit for letting me go. So, anyway, not everyone in a sniper platoon grows up in the Southwest or other rural parts of the U.S., hunting and riding on horseback; although we had those guys in our platoon.

(In my preface I talked about how I met with a Marine Corps Scout Sniper, Rory, who had to vet my legitimacy before he networked me into the sniper community, and how before meeting him I had this mental image of what he would look like, a stereotyped image. I felt bad for stereotyping, even though I wouldn't have let it negatively influence my interpersonal communication with Rory. I train different types of investigators and intelligence professionals to this day in enhanced communication skills. Part of what I teach focuses on getting rid of your biases, prejudices, and assumptions when you meet people and when conducting interrogations and interviews, because it may negatively affect the outcome in the rapport you are trying to build and the information you are trying to collect. So the fact that Rory didn't look like that, or even if he did, played no part in how I communicated with him. (I especially don't feel bad now, because even snipers have a stereotyped mental image of what a sniper should look like!)

We were all on a first-name basis, which is very uncommon in an infantry unit because of the discipline needed to carry out infantry operations. But because of the types of missions snipers do, you could be a sergeant having a conversation with a lance corporal on a first-name basis. People may not realize using someone's first name is important because it signifies a personal relationship and trust that extends beyond strict military discipline in an infantry battalion.

We trained pretty hard, always shooting, always moving, always doing some type of training that pushes your limits physically and mentally leading up to our deployments. Shoot, move, communicate, medicate—that's what we say. We did a lot of urban tactics because we knew we were going to Fallujah. Our sister platoons, 2/4 and 2/5, were already in Ramadi, and they were taking casualties; it was like we were on deck while the guys at bat were getting hammered. I remember when the Marines from those battalions came back from Iraq, there were sixty-man Purple Heart formations. So I was a new platoon sergeant, haven't gone to OIF, watching these guys in formation on crutches, in wheelchairs, guys all bandaged up, guys with eye patches, it was unbelievable. And my buddy Tim (La Sage), who I respected because of his experience and combat leadership, was one of those statistics.

You know prior to OIF (Operation Iraqi Freedom), having snipers get killed was almost unheard of. There was this feeling of invincibility if you were a sniper. We never made contact; we broke it. You shoot and then you're out. We observe and no one ever sees us. There was no insurgency at that time, no IEDs, no suicide bombers, so guys would come back all pumped up and were like, "Dude, we killed a lot of fucking people." Don't get me wrong; we lost Marines during the initial invasion. But there was this sense of pride and accomplishment created when 5th Marines, one of the most decorated regiments in the Marine Corps, returned with another battle streamer. So we were riding that wave of combat success while training in a regiment with that mindset, until the events in Ramadi happened, and it was like, "oh fuck."

CARNAGE IN RAMADI

"What is interesting to me now, is looking back and understanding the political situation of that time. In early 2004 the Iraqi insurgency wasn't 'commonplace' yet, prior to the Blackwater incident. We remember the initial push to Baghdad where we lost Marines, there was a lot of fighting, but once the Marines transitioned south of Baghdad, things got relatively quiet. There was some sporadic fighting, but guys on the ground said it was pretty mundane. We thought the war was over at that point. But then the Iraqi Sunni insurgency exploded in the west in Al Anbar province, which happened to be the same place that we were being deployed to. The notion of OIF '2' was kind of out there; we still thought that by the time we get to Al Anbar the fighting would be over and we would be in more of a transition period; going from war to peacekeeping. We were so wrong."

Within Fritz's regiment there were two famous, or I should say infamous, incidences that happened in his sister platoons. Here is a quick lesson on military organization: typically in the Marine Corps infantry you have the rule of threes; a regiment is comprised of three battalions; a battalion is comprised of three line (infantry) companies, with one weapons company and one headquarters company; and a company is comprised of three line platoons and one weapons platoon. "In sniper platoons the military organization is set up a little differently. My regiment was different in that there were four battalions instead of three, called a reinforced regiment, making four sniper platoons throughout the regiment, so one sniper platoon per battalion and four battalions in the regiment. Depending on what platoon you were in, you were either in a sniper team or sniper section; semantics. There is one sniper team per company. So in a sniper platoon you have a core group of Marines broken up into six teams, and they all push to the companies, one team per company. Four sniper teams are direct support to the three line companies and the heavy weapons company, and then four teams are in general support of the entire battalion's mission." Fritz was one of the platoon sergeants for one of the four sniper platoons within the regiment, and not all four deploy at the same time; they rotate. So at this point, spring of 2004, Fritz was still stateside with his sniper platoon at Camp Pendleton. "Sniper teams have the flexibility of organizing their teams to their needs; some are six-man teams, some are four-man teams, and some are two-man teams, situation dependent. 2/4 decided to organize into a two-man sniper team and were augmented by two line Marines, so they became a four-man team, but only two were trained snipers. So in essence the twenty-four-man platoon now became a forty-eight-man platoon; they doubled down on personnel. The idea for this organization was that the two Scout Snipers could do their piece (do what they were trained to do as a sniper) and the two line Marines could provide security for them. So it's spring 2004, in Ramadi, and the battalion that was there found themselves in precarious situations, many times, for lots of reason. One particular incident involved a four-man sniper team who were gunned downed and killed in broad daylight at their observation post on the rooftop of an Iraqi's house. This left the Marines in shock and the Marine Corps wondering how the enemy could have snuck up on four highly trained Marines, two of which who were supposed to be trained Marine Corps Scout Snipers, in broad daylight and ambushed them. Having an entire sniper team killed was unimaginable. The training they had all been through leading up to deployment and because of the general situation on the ground, which again, seemed like the war and fighting was winding down, not ramping up, left everyone thunderstruck. I remember saying to myself, 'This was getting real.' Snipers are the most highly trained Marines; how could an entire team be killed? That was an eye-opener."

According to an article by Christian Lowe, a *Marine Corps Times* staff writer, "Rooftop Execution, NCIS report provides details of sniper deaths" (http://www.snipercountry.com/Articles/SIA_RooftopExecution .asp), there was only one school-trained sniper on that team. He stated that the four-man team set up their overwatch on a two-story house owned by a local family in Ramadi that was undergoing construction. The family had apparently consented to their presence on the roof. The team had been calling in situation reports (SITREPs) every thirty minutes until fifty-one minutes went by without SITREP. A foot patrol was sent out to their observation post to check on the team, figuring their com-

munications went down. They never imagined they would find the car-
nage that they did once they arrived. The rooftop was covered in blood,
and four dead Marines lay there pierced with bullet holes. Theories and
RUMINT (a slang term we use in the intelligence field that stands for
"rumor intelligence," meaning uncorroborated information for which
you have no idea of the veracity or legitimacy) spread like wildfire about
how this happened: Was it because the four-man team went on a 50
percent security, meaning two slept while two maintained watch? Was it
because there was only one trained sniper and not two, or perhaps they
became complacent with the homeowners and the construction workers
going in and out of the home throughout the day? The Naval Criminal
Investigative Service (NCIS) conducted a thorough investigation. The
results, stated in this article, suggest that the causing factor was that four
enemy combatants posed as construction workers that day, entered the
house, went to the rooftop, and took the Marines by surprise. The sniper
community took a big hit regarding their training practices.

The second incident that happened with another sister battalion's
sniper platoon was while they were conducting a ground patrol. They
had just been inserted in Ramadi by a vehicle. Two of the Marines in 2/5
bounded down an alleyway, and then three got ready to follow. Just as
the three Marines stepped out into the street, they set off a daisy chain
IED in the road, which killed two of them instantly. (The surviving
sniper was Timothy La Sage.)

> What was really disturbing about this incident was that these two par-
> ticular Marines had been best friends since birth; they grew up together,
> and they died together in combat. They went to boot camp together,
> School of Infantry together, they were both in the same sniper platoon
> together; basically, they held hands together through their short career
> and then died together. Even their families were very close. That was a
> hard situation to digest, because first, it was another hit to the regimen-
> tal sniper platoons, and second, it made me realize that same situation
> could happen in my platoon, because I paired team members up with
> their buddies. I thought that being so close and having to work like we
> do, as a tight-knit family, pairing up snipers who knew each other would
> be beneficial for team cohesiveness, but that event made me think dif-
> ferently. Snipers are a little bit different from the line platoon because
> in a four-man team, no matter what your rank is, those four individuals
> carry the same amount of responsibility and weight load, and everybody

is expected to carry 25 percent of the load. Not like in an infantry squad, where you have thirteen to fourteen Marines, or an infantry platoon, where you have thirty-five to forty Marines, where the responsibility is on the leadership, the team leaders, and squad leaders, etc., not on every individual member. What my idea initially was going into my billet as platoon sergeant was to put those Marines who already had relationships built with one another together in a four-man sniper team. But when our sister platoon got hit and those two Marines died together, our platoon was impacted pretty hard. I had grouped together friends, basically. So I had to make a hard call to split one particular team up because there were two Marines, again, who were raised together, who were best friends, grew up in Washington State together, gone through training together, neither one a school-trained sniper; they were PIGs. But after what had just happened, I didn't want the same thing happening to them. It wasn't because I didn't trust them or their ability to accomplish the mission, it was because of the potential impact it would have on their friends and especially these two Marines' families at home. It was a tough call, but I had to split them up. Luckily I had plenty of good snipers and trained combat vets who weren't snipers in the platoon to backfill and take their place going into OIF 2B, which is now more well known as Operation Phantom Fury in Fallujah.

Training at this time changed too. We had to become reactive to what was going on in Iraq. I was using my CQB training, anything relevant from my infantry squad tactics, to try and roll into sniper training. I was trying to keep up with the times, with what was going on over in Iraq, to best prepare my Marines. Watching what these guys went through when they returned really made me think. I saw Tim (La Sage) when he got back, and I saw what happened to his leg. He lost a good portion of his leg, but his femoral artery was still intact; it was like some weird divine intervention.

(Fritz agreed with me that he shouldn't be living.)

IT WAS A TYPICAL CAMP PENDLETON NIGHT; THE STARS LITTERED THE SKY

Still in Camp Pendleton:

It was SOP (standard operation procedure) in our platoon, not officially, rather unofficially, that every Friday as soon as possible, after work, all the Marines and our family members would go to the beach on Camp Pendleton for a barbecue. I have a lot of great memories and pictures from those good times of all of us goofing off on beach, cooking food and watching sunsets over the Pacific, playing guitar; building that brotherhood in our platoon. We were all family and were aware of the dangers that lie ahead of us for our upcoming deployment to Iraq from hearing about those two incidents I mentioned earlier and watching the news as the Iraqi insurgency was growing. We knew we were going into a pretty harsh situation, and our families knew it as well.

The night we left is probably out of all things from my years in the Marine Corps the most vivid memory I have. It was a typical Camp Pendleton night; the stars littered the sky, it was a cooler night, maybe fifty-five degrees, we were all in the parking lot inside Camp Pendleton where we deploy from, where the buses pick us up and transport us to a military flight heading overseas. We had staged all of our weapons, our sea bags, and our personal gear. You generally wait around for a couple of hours, packing, organizing, and saying goodbyes. And even though we were getting ready to leave our families for six months and deploy to a war zone, there wasn't this sense of foreboding and sorrow; that parking lot was almost a festive environment. This was 2004, when patriotism was running high even in OIF, generally speaking; sure, there were protests and political sensitivities in the news, but generally, it was a time of patriotism, and we were ready to do the job. I had confidence in my Marines. We had built a strong relationship with the battalion and the companies we would be supporting, and we were tasked to go to Iraq and kill people. It was simple. And obviously do our job as scouts for the battalion. We would be the eyes and ears for the battalion, but at the end of the day we were trained and equipped to kill Iraqi insurgents, and that's what we were going to do. We had an ad-hoc informal ceremony where the HOGs of the platoon presented the PIGs with a PIGs tooth just as a finishing acceptance in the platoon and letting them know that we were going to battle with them. If you don't know, a HOGs tooth is a bullet worn on a piece of 550 green cord; sometimes we use this cord for our shoelaces, but it's an all-purpose rope or cord with a 762 bullet hanging off it, "the tooth." There's some mystery about what the HOGs tooth represents, but simply put, that's the bullet that is meant for you, it designates you as a sniper, gives you good luck; it's almost like a talisman in the battlefield. Well, we had made PIGs teeth out of 556 bullets, a smaller bullet you would shoot out of your M16 or M4, for the PIGs to wear into combat with us. It was a great ceremony; we were so happy to do it. I remember all the families being there vividly. My mom even made a go-to-war poster which said, "Give 'em Hell, Snipers," and it was on our packs, and it was kind of one of those mental things that gives you more "umph" to go off to war, not knowing if you're coming back, but even so, your families stand behind you. And although the families kept an upbeat attitude and everyone supported us emotionally and mentally, there were tears flowing from both sides, from the Marines and from the families. I remember right before I got on the bus to leave, my wife was holding our son, God he was little, about six or seven months old. He was wearing a blue onesie with a white and blue cap on his head, a little beanie, and he was just the most beautiful little boy, and obviously he didn't know what was going on. But when I kissed him and my wife goodbye to get on the bus to be taken to the air force field where I would board the plane taking us overseas, it was probably the hardest moment of my life. It was harder than any training I've done, any previous deployment I've done, and it was, uh, tough. My mindset was that I might never see my boy again. Once I stepped on that bus, I told myself, it's time to go to work, and if it required losing my life, I was prepared to do that. I had just made and was rearing this perfect little human being the past six months and kissing him goodbye at that moment, which I thought might be the last time; it was almost unbearable. We got on the bus. It was nighttime, the windows were tinted, and I remember seeing my wife holding my son; my mom, obviously, was pretty emotional, because it was my first combat tour, and I was her last son. I had a brother who passed away when I was in the ninth grade. She was divorced and living by herself, and I was her baby now going off to war. So there were a couple of emotional experiences going on at once there. And lo and behold, I can say that on the way to the air force base which was about an hour away, I cried the entire time. I don't think anyone ever saw it because I kept my sunglasses on, in the middle of the night. I was trying to keep it together because I was the platoon sergeant specifically tasked to go down range and lead my Marines into combat, but it really drove home the emotion that goes into deployments. The Marine Corps prepares you to kill the enemy, but it doesn't prepare you for leaving your family and potentially never seeing them again.

LESSONS IN LEADERSHIP

I talked about shoot, move, communicate, medicate earlier, and during times when we were training, we had "white space" to fill when there wasn't range training going on or an exercise. I had things to fill in the white space, but my corpsman told me one day, no, he was going to take the guys and train them in trauma medicine. And I was like, 'Right on, Doc.' Fast-forward to Fallujah, November 2004, Phantom Fury, we are in the fight now. The companies are pushing north to south through the city, and one of my sniper teams was pushing with one of the line companies. One of the line Marines in the FLOT (Forward Line of Troops) got hit and went down; he got shot in the head and was trapped in a room in one of the houses on this particular street. He was one house ahead of the sniper team, and there were bad guys in the house next to the one the Marine was trapped in. The sniper team had maneuvered to a rooftop trying to gain a tactical advantage on the insurgents who killed that Marine so they could go in and get him. Three snipers were on the rooftop and the platoon corpsman was with them. As the corpsman was coming down off the rooftop, like a perch, the insurgents shot him nine times with an AK-47. He took four shots across his chest plate, which stopped the bullets; one shot to the nut protector (we call it the nut protector, it's the piece of armor that hangs down), and that stopped; and four shots to his legs. He crumbles to the ground. So the platoon corpsman is the one who gets hurt. One of the guys on the team went over and started working on him, putting tourniquets on his legs; he was one one of the guys the corpsman had trained while they were back in the States prior to their deployment. A very young lance corporal ended up saving the corpsman's life from the training he gave him months earlier. It's not supposed to happen that way. Nobody plans for the corpsman to get hit. Training paid off, a life was saved, and it had nothing to do with shooting people.

Had the platoon corpsman not taken the initiative to train the platoon in trauma medicine, he may not have lived. What comes around goes around, this time in a lifesaving way.

While I was deployed to Fallujah, I learned a lesson in leadership. I was back at our battalion jump area in the northwest end of Fallujah, which is where the COC (Command Operations Center) was at, the detainee handlings were, and where the CASEVACs (casualty evacuations) were coming in. CASEVACs would bring the wounded out of the city to the jump area, and the helicopters would come and take them out of there. So someone told me, hey, your corpsman's coming back, he's hit, and I was like holy shit. We lived across the street from each other in California, so our wives lived across the street from each other. So I'm waiting for him in the rear. All these amtracks come screaming in; I didn't know which one he was in. The ramp dropped on one, and all I saw was his bare feet facing me, tourniquets on his bare legs, because they had cut off his pants, his genitalia, then his face and blood everywhere. He looked at me and I said to him, "Hey, man, you're doing good, we're gonna get you outta here, everything is going to be alright." He said, "Okay," but he kept looking at me, and I kept telling him it was going to be okay. We end up carrying him on a stretcher to a helicopter, and he goes away. I don't see him for months. When I finally meet back up with him after the deployment, he said he wanted to talk to me about something. We were close, we were friends, so I was like, sure man, what's up? He tells me, "I want you to know that you scared the shit out of me that day." I was like, "What do you mean?" He said when the ramp came down on the amtrack that day, he was looking at me because he needed to know he was going to be ok. But when he saw the look on my face, it scared the shit out of him. I felt awful; I didn't even have anything to say to him. I didn't even know I projected that, and I let him down. My look of shock, which I felt but thought I hid, was exactly what he didn't need to see. You never stop learning. I was ready to jump into action; I wasn't thinking of anything else. In my heart and my mind I meant all the right things, but I didn't project it. So that was a leadership lesson I learned that day: being that presence of security and comfort is critical for your men.

PERSEVERANCE THROUGH ADVERSITY

Combat is adversity. Being away from your family is adversity; you appreciate life a little more when you experience adversity. Once you've been through that, everything else is small potatoes, as cliché as it sounds. My wife and I have been married for fifteen years and we are going to grow old together, but it hasn't been perfect. The hardships we've been through have provided us a context, or better perspective on life, which reminds us not to take any day that we are together for granted. I am definitely more reflective these days, not reactive. I preach more about the quality of life and acceptance; I've learned to listen more than talk. If you talked to guys who knew me back then, they would say I was this cocky, egotistical Marine. In fact I recall one specific time when my cockiness and ego were put in check, by me. It was adversity in the sense that I had to swallow my pride because I learned something that day. It was two weeks before we went into Fallujah, and we were ordered to cease outside communications with our families for operational security reasons. We had all started writing "death letters." You have to remember at that time going into an urban environment we were being told there were 90 percent casualties (that was doctrine); that means 10 percent come back with the same amount of holes they went over with. We were mentally convinced that the majority of us wouldn't be coming back. Thankfully we proved that wrong. One day I had the opportunity to run around with a SEAL team. One of they guys I went through boot camp and Sniper School with got out of the Marine Corps and went on to become a SEAL. Well, he ends up being in Fallujah attached to our battalion. So he invited me to go along with them for the day. They had a ranger, who was a master sergeant, attached to their platoon; they just called him "Ranger." So we were entering houses on the outskirts of Fallujah looking for bad guys who had left the city. I'm a young staff sergeant rolling around with SEALs, kicking in doors; it was awesome. In one of the houses we entered, was a family. They were sitting there all freaked out. I have my glasses and helmet on, I got my rifle in my hand, I look like the terminator, and I'm giving this family a hard stare. I didn't interact with the local population at that time, because as infantry we had to maintain a high security posture; it was Fallujah, after all. So Ranger comes up, immediately kneels down, takes his helmet and glasses off, and starts talking to the kids and giving them candy. So in the midst of all this chaos with the SEALs, this dude just rolls up and is making it happen. The kids are now laughing, and he's patting them on the head, calming them down. And I was like, oh, that's what I should be doing; this is what we should be doing. My moment of clarity.

I told Fritz, it's all about being human. It's something I have learned along the way in my career that led to my success as a military interrogator. He replied,

Ya, that's it, I learned I can be human there; I didn't have to be a machine. I was taking stuff so seriously, but then I got the clarity that I can be a sniper and human on the battlefield. When I saw "Ranger," I told myself, I have to be that guy.

Here's what I tell people: the definition of luck is when preparation and opportunity meet. The definition of success is when luck happens and you are willing to step outside your comfort zone. So preparation and opportunity allow you to do some cool stuff, but to actually be successful is when you are willing to push yourself out of your comfort zone. You have to be ready to get extremely uncomfortable, physically and mentally, to be successful in life, which is especially the truth in a job like sniping. I've learned to step outside my comfort zone because of my experiences as a sniper. You push yourself so hard as a sniper. For example, during Hell Week in Sniper School, which was five days long, I had one MRE and four hours of sleep. We had two Navy SEALs in our class at Sniper School, and they were like, "What in the hell is going on right now?" They had been through BUD/S [Basic Underwater Demolition/SEAL school] and their famous Hell Week, and they were even like, "This is not cool." The mental perseverance was brutal. It's almost like an out-of-body experience; you mentally detach. The sniper community lets you know that your mind will shut down much earlier than your body. There are a lot of times I surprised myself with my perseverance, and it has definitely shaped who I am today, personally and professionally.

6

THE WARRIOR SPIRIT
AND MY BROTHERHOOD

As you know by now, I like to quote the snipers that I have interviewed word for word. I like to use their words, not mine, so you can get a feel for the person who is sharing their story with you. As you read this story, you will notice that Zane, the sniper, uses the word *fuck* a lot. And although some of you reading this may find it offensive, neither he nor I mean to offend in any way. That is how Zane talks, and I personally wasn't offended, which is why I didn't change his words. In fact, I read somewhere that people who swear a lot are more honest, which must mean I am also very honest. So here is Zane's very honest account of his time in the United States Marine Corps as a PIG and a HOG.

Zane joined the Marine Corps on July 14, 2008, when he was eighteen. He went in to be a grunt because his older brother was a grunt. (The term *grunt* refers to a military member who's in the infantry. In the Marine Corps, that is anyone whose Military Occupational Specialty [MOS] is preceded by the number 03. For example, an MOS 0311— Basic Rifleman is a grunt, infantry, and a rifleman.)

The only things I really knew about the Marine Corps were the recondos [slang term for people in reconnaissance: inspecting, exploring, and gathering intelligence and information on an area before going into it] and snipers; I didn't really know about regular infantry or pogues [a slightly derogatory Marine Corps term that stands for "people other than grunts" (POG) but pronounced *pogue*]; all I knew were the pipe hitters [slang for "operators," which is a military term for a person who is highly trained to carry out special operations], and that's what I always wanted to be. I grew up in a hunting and shooting environment. Guns and killing were second nature, so it didn't seem like it would be that difficult to do in the Marine Corps. Obviously a deer isn't rocking a PKM (Soviet machine gun) at you, but the idea of smoking bad dudes for ol' glory and getting paid for it seemed pretty legit. Once I graduated boot camp and School of Infantry (SOI) and got to my Battalion, 3rd Battalion, 7th Marines, (3/7) out of Twentynine Palms, California ["Twentynine Palms" refers to the Marine Corps Air Ground Combat Center (MCAGCC) located in Twentynine Palms, California], about a month later I ran the sniper indoc with my best friend Billy, who I grew up with. We went to high school together, joined the Marines together, went through boot camp together, SOI together, and then I talked him into going to the sniper indoc with me. I don't remember if it was a week or two weeks long, but it sucked. I hadn't experienced anything like that yet in my life; we got really thrashed for those two weeks, but it was worth it, and it was exactly what I wanted. And, of course, everyone volunteers to go through that experience, so you want to be there. I wanted to be with a group of people who wanted more, who wanted to be where they were, and who wanted to excel in their job; they were the top level. Since I wasn't in the position to try out for MARSOC [Marine Corps Forces Special Operations Command], because I was a brand-new Marine, my next step up, you could say, was to go to the sniper platoon. Once Billy and I made the platoon, we went to Bridgeport, California, to do our mountain warfare training. From there, I fell on a school slot [Scout Sniper School] as a boot PIG ["boot" meaning junior]. Five of us from went to see if we could get slots in the school, and I was one of the dudes they told to stay. I was used to the regimented Marine Corps; I was saying "Sir" to everyone I passed and getting a knife handed back. I remember when I got to Scout Sniper School, this dude rolled up with long hair, and he had two full sleeves of tattoos; he was a MARSOC staff sergeant and I was like, "Hey, Staff Sergeant, how's it going?" He was so chill, and he says, "No, man, my name is John. It's nice to meet you." [John is an alias name.] He held out his hand for me to shake, and as a boot lance corporal, I didn't understand why this guy was treating me with respect. No senior had given a junior much respect up to this point, and the dude that does was a MARSOC cat who had been on numerous pumps [slang for deployments]. I realized then that these were the right people to be around. You act like a man; you get treated like a man. You act like a bitch; you get treated as such. I dug that.

Zane ended up getting dropped from Sniper School after about five weeks. He failed the known distance shooting qualification three times, and each time by one point. You had to get 28 shots out of 32, and he got 27 on his pre-qual (short for qualification), 27 on his qual, and 27 on his re-qual; at least he was consistent.

"I was so torn up. I really wanted to be a sniper and I was proud to be doing it, even though I was a young boot PIG. I had a lot of pride in becoming a sniper. Gunny L [initials will be used to protect the identities of people throughout the story], a very well respected HOG on the West Coast, who had come over to my platoon for a short period of time, came to pick me up at the Schoolhouse in Camp Pendleton to drive me back to Twentynine Palms after I had been dropped. I remember when he showed up, I was actually crying and apologized to him for failing and he was like, 'You're fine.' He knew I really cared about being a HOG, and he knew it was something I really wanted. He told me, 'You'll probably have another shot at it.' When I heard him say that, I was immediately motivated to work harder and to get back there."

After getting dropped from Sniper School, Zane returned to his sniper platoon and went to Mojave Viper, still as a PIG, with hopes of getting a second shot at going back to Scout Sniper School, passing, and becoming a HOG. Mojave Viper was a thirty-day predeployment training exercise "that trains active duty and Reserve Fleet Marine Force units and Marine Air Ground Task Forces (MAGTF) in command, control, and coordination of kinetic and nonkinetic fires in the 'Three Block War.'" Mojave Viper is the most realistic, live-fire training exercise in the Marine Corps. It provides the commanders the opportunity to employ all the capabilities of the MAGTF. Approximately two thousand Marines and sailors participate in each training cycle, which uses the "building block" approach, starting with small-unit training and culminating with MAGTF integration (http://www.militarynew comers.com/29palms/resources/03_mission.html). After Mojave Viper, Zane was sent to Mountain Communications School in Bridgeport, California. While there, he had an altercation with a sergeant who was stationed there. "This pogue sergeant called me a PIG and said we were going to die in Afghanistan." I was shocked when Zane said this and asked him why on earth this guy would ever say such a terrible thing. "Fuck if I know. So I called him a fat fuck or fat fucking pogue, or something like that. So of course his command told my command and the Bridgeport sergeant major reported it to my battalion sergeant major, and so my battalion sergeant major took me out of the sniper platoon. I got placed in CAAT [Combined Anti-Armor Team] White, which is the mobile CAAT team in weapons company. I was so pissed, and I was an angry person as it was. Growing up in Dallas, Texas, I was raised in a very aggressive family. My father was aggressive; fighting was normal for me. Before I got out of high school I had been in about fifty street fights. And so already having this base demeanor, when I got put in CAAT, I became very disgruntled, and I was like 'Fuck CAAT White, I don't want to be here.' I felt like everyone in my platoon were shit hot guys, and now I'm with a bunch of window lickers." Zane was stuck in CAAT White and sucked it up. He deployed as a member of CAAT White at the end of March 2010.

MUSA QALA 1 AND 2

"I can't remember where we got told we were going; it was to Afghanistan, but we didn't know where exactly. There was only about fifteen or sixteen of us, originally, in the entire sniper platoon, so it was a small platoon. We ended up being split into two teams once we got there." This is significant later on, and you'll see why. Zane landed in Afghanistan and checked in to Camp Leatherneck. Camp Leatherneck is an ISAF military base in the Washir district of Helmand province, now under Afghan control since 2014. From there he and his platoon drove up to Forward Operation Base Delaram, Camp Delaram, a military expeditionary base built by the United States Marine Corps. The Afghan National Army now occupies and controls the base. "While I was with CAAT, I picked up shifts as a radio operator. I was filling all of the radios in the trucks with crypto [encryption devices] and making sure everything was up to par in case we had to role on a Quick Reaction Force (QRF) mission. I remember I was trying to do everything I could to get back to the sniper platoon. The platoon commander told the CO (Commanding Officer) that I was working hard, and Gunny O, who was the platoon sergeant then, told me some of the best advice I have ever received. Right when I showed up, he said, 'Zane, you want to go back to STA Platoon, right? [STA Platoon is an acronym that stands for stands for Surveillance, Target, and Acquisition Platoon; the home of Marine Corps Scout Snipers.] Well, remember, make yourself an asset, not a liability.' And then he said, 'And as of right now, you're here, not in STA, so do what you can to show us you should go back.'" Zane took those words to heart. At that point he had been in Delaram, in Helmand province, for about a month with CAAT White. They had been running long-distance driving missions out of that base to Washir, another village in the Helmand province, and Buji Bhast Pass, which is a pass through the Buji Bhast Mountains in Farah province in southern Afghanistan. Buji Bhast Pass was a Taliban stronghold and littered with their IEDs.

> They were bullshit missions where nothing was going on. Both the CAAT teams and sniper teams weren't doing much. We were pushing into Washir and Musa Qala, and that's when things starting popping off. At that time I was told they were going to let me go back to my sniper platoon, and I was super stoked. But at that time I was still with CAAT. When shit started popping off, it was fucking gnarly. It was the first firefights anyone in 3/7 were getting into; for the snipers, CAAT Red, and the squads. My element of CAAT White hadn't experience combat. Musa Qala was right up on the Helmand river valley, so it was desert that went right up into the green zone, the vegetated area. There were a lot of Taliban in the area . . . a lot of foreign fighters too. As my element was driving over the hills into the green zone, the truck I was driving rolled. My element had to hold up there for a couple days before continuing the mission. Once we linked up with everyone, a lot of shit had popped off already. We finished the rest of that clearing op (clearing Taliban out of the area), which lasted another few days, and then rolled back to Delaram.

As soon as Zane got back from Musa Qala, which we'll call Musa Qala 1, as this was the first push into Musa Qala and there would be a second, he went back to join his sniper platoon; he was still in Delaram. He joined back up with his buddies, who by now all had combat experience.

> We're about to push out to Musa Qala again for the second push, and my buddies were seasoned and ready to get back into the fight. Here I

am, fresh, I don't know what the fuck is going to happen, I hadn't seen combat yet. We were split into two teams; the platoon sergeant at the time split us up into two eight-man teams. Shadow, our call sign, Two, was in the front of the push and we (Shadow One) were on the back side of the push where the clearing started; it was a Taliban stronghold. My best friend Bill was in Shadow Two, and I always wanted to be on his team, but we were split. When the push started, the trucks were hitting IED after IED from the get-go. They were going through a valley, and there was a danger area in the valley on the way up the hill to Musa Qala. Truck after truck hit IEDs there, about ten or eleven within twenty-four hours in that particular valley that led to Musa Qala. Kilo Company, and I think the battalion PSD (Personal Security Detachment), kept trying to push through the same spot, and they wanted to clear out this area. That's when Corporal Q went out and found an IED in this valley. My buddy and I were sitting in our position, and we hear them call out an IED position over the radio. So we see Corporal Q about a hundred meters away in the valley going over to this IED to mark it with a bottle cap so EOD (Explosives and Ordinance Disposal) could come clear it later. It was over a hundred-pound IED. As he went to mark it, it went off. It just pink misted him. He fucking disappeared. Completely blew him the fuck up. I mean, there wasn't a leg, nothing. Caleb and I watched this happen. That was the first realization for me that oh fuck, life can be taken from you real quick. Everything that your parents put in to make you and everything that you do in life can evaporate that fast. So for me, when that happened, I realized death is a reality, this place ain't a fucking game, this place ain't no joke, this shit is real as fuck. It was definitely a reality check for me. A couple of guys went out to collect him, and let's just say there wasn't much left of him to collect.

Shadow Two continued to push into Musa Qala, and they started getting it. This was a two-week, or ten-day, mission. We were on the back side of this mission to make sure the enemy didn't back lay IEDs after we cleared them so everyone could have a safe route of exit to push back through on the way out, after they retreated from Musa Qala. That was supposedly our mission.

Meanwhile, Shadow Two had advanced to Musa Qala. Shadow One, Zane's team, were still on the other side of the valley on the back side of a hill watching, waiting, and hearing tons of fire coming over the radios.

Shadow Two was smoking a fuck ton of dudes. This was going on for days. We hadn't really seen shit at all. All we were hearing was the kinetic gunfire from a couple of clicks away from our sister team; we didn't really have a clue as to what was going on. A buddy of mine from one of the CAAT teams rolled up in a truck to resupply us a couple of days into it, and I remember me and my buddy Ben went up to him in the truck, and he asked us if we had heard what happened to Patino. We were like, what are you talking about? He said, "Patino's dead." We were like, what the fuck are you talking about? Patino was the assistant team leader of our sister team, Shadow Two. This guy was the most badass sniper there ever was by all means. Patino came over from 1/5 (1st Battalion, 5th Marines) previously. He was on deployment, came back, crossed over units to deploy again with us; he was a combat veteran and solid as fuck. He was the type of dude that every sniper would meet, or anyone would meet and you immediately looked up to the guy; he was a stud. When I got put back in the platoon, after being kicked out and sent to CAAT White, the platoon sergeant at that time was pretty shitty towards me, but this dude, Claudio Patino, was there for me. He wanted to train me and make me better.

At this point I tell Zane about a personal experience that I wrote about in my previous book that has to do with true and professed confidence. My quote: "True confidence is the mentor, professed confidence is the aggressor," meaning, people who have true confidence don't feel they have to prove it to you. Instead they share their knowledge with you, mentor you, and listen to you. People who profess they have confidence will try to convince you of that by becoming aggressive and disrespectful. They are too concerned with someone seeing through their false pretenses shielding their lack of self-confidence, so they become paranoid that they will be overthrown in their position of authority and defend it aggressively. They do not listen to others or take advice for fear of looking inferior; almost like a feared leader. They do not respect their subordinates and hence lose respect from their subordinates. Just as with liars, they try to convince you of information sometimes by bullying and being aggressive. Truthful people convey information because they have nothing to hide or prove. Zane smiled and shook his head in agreement.

Absolutely. The platoon sergeant wasn't a confident person; he thought he had a lot of shit to prove. Patino was super knowledgeable, super badass, and he was wicked in combat. We heard what he did in Musa Qala 1, which was kill a ton of enemy fighters, with everyone else in

Shadow Two, so when Ben and I found out he got killed, we were like what the fuck! How is that possible? It was crazy to have someone you looked up to and idolized end up dead. He was our first KIA, and three other dudes had been medevaced: Croft, who was our team leader; Mac, who was one of my best friends, crazy motherfucker; and Nick, all had been medevaced. So we just hear all of this and we're in shock, and our platoon sergeant knew shit was going on but never told us. He obviously had to know, he's on the radio with them and he can hear who's being medevaced, who's engaging in contact with enemy, and he's not telling anyone what the fuck is going on. We immediately walked up to him, and he could tell we knew something was going on. As we asked him what the fuck was going on with Shadow Two. He decided to spill the beans. He told the eight of us up on the hill what had happened. Since we were in eight-man teams, the other team was now down to four. He had known; he just didn't want to tell everyone. I don't know his mindset, cause I can't think like that; I'm not that type of man. But I'll never understand his idea on why he didn't want to tell us. So we had no idea what was going on with them. All we knew was our sister team was fucked up on the other side of the hill just a few clicks away. And everyone on my team was asking why the fuck aren't we doing anything right now to help them? Why aren't we moving?

I ask Zane what it felt like to hear that your sister team is in heavy combat, has lost half of their team members, and you are sitting with your team on a hill waiting, not able to assist?

It was the worst fucking feeling in the world. I mean, really, when I was there, I guess I didn't have the balls to get up and say, I'm rolling on my own. The platoon sergeant said the battalion commander said we couldn't move. But I remember saying, we need to fucking support them, and I was the youngest dude on the team, but I was like, we can't just leave them out there, we need to at least try to do something. But the platoon sergeant kept saying to us that we needed to stay in our position because that was the battalion commander's order. Fuck the battalion commander's orders! We should have helped them. That is something I've had to deal with over time. A lot of my close friends were out there getting fucked up, and we weren't doing anything.

On the exfil [short for exfiltration, or extraction] from Musa Qala, there were a ton of enemy mortar positions set up; they dropped like seventy-two mortars on the Kilo position within minutes. [Kilo is a unit

designation for an infantry company.] The Kilo position was where all
the vehicles were staged to take us out of Musa Qala and back to the
main base in Delaram. We packed up and ran to the trucks, loaded onto
the trucks, and dipped out. Lots of people in Kilo around those trucks
took shrapnel. I remember when we got back to Delaram, our team got
in there, none of us who had been in combat, and then the other team,
Shadow Two, got there, and they had already been on two intense runs.
Now there were only four of them left. They weren't in just a couple of
firefights; they were in firefights for days on end for weeks, constantly
engaging. They probably killed over 100 dudes in Musa Qala alone; eight
dudes killed over 100 in those few weeks. I'll never forget seeing Billy's
face when he got back to base and walked into our hooch [Billy was on
Shadow Two]. I was like [Zane paused a lot, trying to think of how to
describe what he felt in words when he tells me this part of his story], it
was super heart wrenching, and I totally felt like we let them down. I felt
that way then, and to this day I still feel it. I had a lot of resentment, and
it took a few years to let it go. I felt really bad. I was sitting with him, and
I told myself I would never let him down like that again. There's no fucking way. Our platoon sergeant ended up going home after that mission,
because he said something was up with his knee and he didn't know if
he'd be good. We all think he ducked out, and we were glad he did. You
knew who wanted to be there and who didn't.

CANCER AND SANGIN

Zane and his platoon were still at Delaram waiting for their next mission: Sangin, a town in Helmand province. According to the *Marine
Corps Times* article, "Into the breach: How Sangin will enter the annals
of Marine history," written by Hope Hodge Seck, on May 12, 2014:

SANGIN, AFGHANISTAN—They had called it "Sangingrad." A full
third of all British casualties in Afghanistan had occurred in the Sangin
district of Helmand Province, and by the time they decided to leave, The
Guardian, one of Britain's most well-read newspapers, said that troops
"applauded" the pullout. The paper also declared the Taliban in Sangin
"undefeated." The namesake comes from Stalingrad, the failed German siege in Russia that turned the tide on the Eastern Front in World
War II. Pound for pound, it's one of the bloodiest battles in the history

of armed conflict. Apparently, the Brits saw parallels to it in Afghanistan. . . . Marine infantry units sustained casualties in Sangin at some
of the highest rates seen over the course of this 13-year war." (http://
archive.marinecorpstimes.com/article/20140512/NEWS/305120018/
Into-breach-How-Sangin-will-enter-annals-Marine-history)

Zane went on to tell me,

The battalion commander told the company commander to let the company take a week off before we pushed on to Sangin. We were before
3/5; they ripped [RIP is a military acronym that stands for Relieve in
Place] us out, we ripped the Brits out. The last week off before we go
into Sangin, I went to the MWR [Morale, Welfare, and Recreation] and
called home. My dad had cancer; I knew that before I went on deployment, and I knew it was bad. My brother, who is a MARSOC Marine and
a sniper, had just gotten off his postdeployment leave a month earlier.
When I called my dad's house, he picked up the phone. I immediately
knew something was wrong. Shit ain't good if my brother is there, because my brother shouldn't be in Texas at my dad's house; he should be
at his home in North Carolina. So I was like, what's up with dad; he told
me, "Dad's about to die." He said I should come home, but I was like
fuck, I ain't coming home. So my sister gets on the phone, and she tells
me I need to come home; I told her I wasn't coming home. So my dad
gets on the phone, and I told my dad, "I'm not coming home." My dad
was supportive of my decision and me. It was my brother and sister who
wanted me to come home. I wasn't going to let my team down; I'm not
dipping out when we are about to roll into a more kinetic spot. I went
back to my hooch after the phone call, sat outside, and lit up a cigarette.
I remember that conversation felt like the biggest kick in the balls. [Zane
lets out a nervous laugh and paused for a bit. I know there are still rem-
nants of what he felt that day that have stayed with him even to this day.]
My buddies Oscar and Billy knew something was up when I walked in the
hooch. So Billy came over to talk to me and asked me what's going on,
and I told him about my dad. I told him not to worry, because I wasn't
going to leave them.

As you read this, you may be thinking, how could he not want go
home to see his dying father? It almost sounds cold and cruel. But that
is not Zane. In fact, as I got to know him throughout this interview, that
is anything but how I would describe him. He is extremely loyal to those

close to him, spiritual, and pure, as you will read later. I can suspect Zane's decision at that time was heavily influenced by the intense feeling he had when he felt he let his sister team down in Musa Qala.

Billy said, dude, you have to go home; you need to go see your dad. I was at a crossroad: do I go home while he's dying or for the burial? The new platoon commander, Jake, he was a great guy, awesome guy, said I should go home too. He was our chief scout, but since one team leader was medavaced and the platoon sergeant dipped out, he took over the platoon. I told him I'm not going home, because I have heard stories about guys who had to go home, and then they get stuck home and can't come back on deployment, so I'm not fucking leaving. Then my CO found out and he was like, "Listen, you're going home." I told him the only way I'm going home was if he guaranteed I'm coming back. I'm not leaving these dudes behind again. I can't remember exactly what he said, but he basically promised me I could come back, so they flew me to Leatherneck; then I flew back home. I got back stateside, and I remember my dad was at home, not in a hospital, and I was like, why did I just fly all the way back here if he's still home? I was pissed off because I had to leave my team to come home and see him being just fine, it seemed like. He ended up being taken to the hospital later that night, and obviously I felt like shit for thinking that way. The next six days I spent in the hospital with my dad, I sat with him every day. There was only one day I think that I didn't sleep in the chair in his room, because my sister forced me to go home and she stayed with him. The last day I was talking to him and I knew, that was it, he was going to hospice and I was going back to Afghanistan. I told him . . .

and at this point Zane clears his throat, pauses, and leans in and word for word recites this quote: "He is not gone who departs from life with a legacy of love left behind him. What lives and grows in the hearts we touch endures to make us immortal." He clapped his hands almost as if in rejoice that he remembered that quote. It is clearly visible that he is still touched by this quote today. And then, he was back on a plane returning to Afghanistan, to a war zone.

August 8th, 2010, which is coming up [at the time of this interview], the day I get back to Afghan, I open up my email and there's an email from my sister that my father has died. It was more of a relief to know that he wasn't in pain. I was like, all right, back to business. I show up my platoon, which was now operating as one team because we had so few guys, and the whole platoon had just had gone through another huge push in Kilo in Sangin. I linked up with them at the end of that. All of Sangin was clearing operations because no one had cleared this area yet. So Kilo was clear, then we were going to do Lima's and India's [unit designations for infantry companies], and then we were going to do our RIP and then head out. They trucked me out to link up with my team. There were ten of us living under a trailer out under the stars on this little-ass base; it was a British patrol base, Folad. Everyone else there were sleeping in racks, but we were the outcasts, so the Lima first sergeant told us we could sleep under the trailer, and I'm talking a baby trailer. One or two of us could actually fit under it, so we just all slept outside. The Brits were getting shot at daily, and the tankers who were trying to build a bridge were getting shot constantly. We were smoking dudes from the roof posts at Folad too. I don't know what led us to do this mission with Lima, but we go out on our first patrol and we get up on this wall of a compound, and this dude launches a water balloon launcher and popped this grenade over at us. Me, Caleb, and Oscar all heard the crack and pop of the water balloon launcher. The grenade hit the wall, then hit Caleb in the shoulder, then lands on the ground right next to him and Oscar. I was like fuck, we are definitely in the kill zone! It was like something you see in the movies. Caleb yelled "grenade" when he saw it in the air, but we didn't expect it to hit us. It became real, real fast. I made two big steps to get away in this muddy cornfield, and I tripped and went facedown in it. The grenade went off, and I took shrapnel in my ribs and my face, on my chin. I was fucking rocked. Caleb was deaf, but I remember him shaking me, screaming "Zane! Zane!" He thought I was dead because my Kevlar was down over my face and I was bleeding out of my chin. I guess I blacked out for a minute but then realized he was yelling at me and I said, "I'm good, I'm good," at least I thought I was, and I hopped up onto my feet. I felt my face and my chin. It felt like I got punched and I was bleeding. I was peppered with a little bit of shrapnel, and my ribs and chest were burning, but I was good, I was fortunate. We checked to make sure we were all good and then we pushed into this house, essentially to get accountability, and immediately we hear, "Hey, snipers, get up on the roof!" and we go up there and immediately start getting slammed with fire. We couldn't figure from where, but then we spotted a machine gun position, and I shot up that position. Bart, another guy, shot up the AK fire position. As soon as we got done taking out those two enemy positions, we pushed back to Folad. We had to patrol back, walking, because we couldn't get medevac vehicles into this area because it was all flooded. We had dudes throwing up from concussions from the grenade, and we had to stop every few minutes for them to throw up. We made it back to Folad, and then they took us to FOB Nolay to see the doctor. The doctor asks me if I have a concussion, and I said, nope, I'm good, I'm ready to go back out. I was the first one in. When the rest of the guys came out they were like yea, we got a week off from patrolling. I was like what the fuck, I just lied so I could patrol, and they were like fuck that, we've been out there every day. We all ended going back out about five days later with India. We did clearings and got into a decent amount of firefights with India.

The last month of their being on their own out in Sangin, an incident happened that was one of Zane's "what-if" moments.

There was this one time we rolled outside the wire, literally, right outside the wire, and this round hits right between me and Pete, and so we turn around and roll back in the wire. It was from a position where this dude kept taking potshots at us. So we decide we are going to set up in his building and wait for him to roll up near his position where he's shooting from so when he comes in the next day, or evening, we are just going to fucking kill him. So we build this position in this abandoned building that had been blown up. It was in a pomegranate orchard that had blown to shit, and all the buildings around it were blown to shit. So we waited for this dude to come in. I remember facing my field of view; my avenue of view is the majority of this courtyard with gates, and this blown-out hole in the wall where dudes can come in and out of. I'm intently watching this area. All of sudden this dude in blue man jammies pops up in my 3 o'clock up on top of the wall about four or five feet away, and I was like, oh shit! He didn't see us because he was looking in the same direction we were, but he is right over us. My gun is lying in my lap and my pistol was on my hip. I went for my gun real quick, and he sees me and hops over the wall fast to get to his motorcycle that was staged there for him. We had heard motorcycles earlier, but he must have killed the engine early because we didn't hear one come that close to our position. We immediately break down the team because we had been compromised, and we get up and exfil out of there. Bart and Mac watched that hole in that house for the next two days, from PB Atul [a British Patrol Base located in Helmand province, Nahri Saraj district], where we had rolled out and taken potshots from. We watched his building from a post on PB Atul waiting for him to come back. He finally came back and ends up taking a shot to the face. I really regretted that decision, to go for my rifle instead of my pistol. I should have just gone for my pistol, because it was right there!

BLOODY MONDAY

"We went on another mission, in Sangin, right after we had linked up with a squad in India; that was a gnarly mission. In fact, some commanders labeled it 'Bloody Monday,' but I don't think it was any crazier than the shit Shadow Two was seeing on a regular basis in Musa Qala. It was a huge firefight with a ton of people. About fifty-four Taliban, I think, had been killed that day, grenades flying back and forth. My buddy who was a machine gunner in India got shot during that op. Our combat cameraman got shot and died on that op; in fact, it was two weeks before he was going home. He had made all his plans with his family, too, to come home." When Zane told me this, all I could think was how his family felt. In fact, I think I zoned out for a minute or two with those thoughts and tuned out everything Zane was saying. Can you imagine as a mother, father, sibling, girlfriend, or friend, speaking and talking to him, making travel plans to pick him up when his flight comes in, organizing a party or celebration with family and friends for his return, cooking his favorite food, preparing the house and linens, fully expecting to give him the biggest hug ever when he gets off the tarmac once he lands, and then all of a sudden, he's taken from you within minutes? I don't know how families survive that loss, but they do, and should be respected and appreciated for being so strong.

> We went in two buildings connected in that compound that had IEDs inside; one had fourteen, the other had ten. Twenty-four IEDs set to blow all of us up when we went in there. There was a fuck ton of IEDs where we were. There were machine guns rockin', they were fighting us with all sorts of weapons. The significance of that day, I believe, was that the Taliban hit every FOB and base that Marines were on in Sangin simultaneously. A whole bunch of grenades were thrown that day at us and at India. And a metric fuck ton of HIMARS (High Mobility Artillery Rocket System] were dropped on those fucks . . . good day. A suicide bomber

rolled up right outside the house we had taken over. He came up on a motorbike where the bomb was intuited with the bike's kill switch. He got off, and as a Marine started to approach him to search him, he blew himself up, and chunks of him flew into the building, haha. He took out the eye of the Marine who went to search him, and that Marine caught shrapnel, but he was pretty fortunate, seeing what could have happen. Fortunately Ol' Terry (Taliban) blew himself up too early! He didn't get any one of us! I tried to get my buddy Brett to eat a piece of him . . . I was like "Fucking do it, Brett! You're a savage." He wouldn't do it. At the time, it was funny, though. [I asked Zane if he seriously wanted Brett to eat a piece of him, and he replied, "Lol, yeah."]

There were a good amount of firefights with that clearing op. After Bloody Monday, 3/5 came in, and we were going to RIP them out and do left seat, right seat and then go home. They came to see how we did things, but it ended up to be hard fucking times for 3/5. For us, 3/7, it started out with potshots in Washir and then to Musa Qala twice, then Sangin three times in a row, monthlong ops, and a countless number of firefights one after another. So 3/5 just got thrown into this op (short for operational) tempo, and they were good guys, but they were taking a shit ton of casualties because these dudes weren't used to it yet, and the Taliban were taking advantage that it was a RIP: old guys leaving, new guys coming in.

I asked Zane if the Taliban knew when they rotated in new units, like they did in GTMO when they knew guard rotations. His reply was, "Ya, they knew. People were always watching us, and the ANA have shit-heads who are definitely working both sides of the field."

I MIGHT AS WELL HAVE BEEN BACK IN AFGHANISTAN

After Zane got back home, he went to his dad's wake; his family held the wake service until Zane got home so he could attend. About a week later, while in Palm Springs, California, a few of Zane's buddies and he went out on the town. "This was like the first week back in civilization. For months we had been living off the land; dudes were killing chickens and goats to eat, we weren't showering, it was a very simple life, it was hard, but simple. So we went out to a bar and three of my guys and me got in an altercation with these nine pogues. It was about the deployment. They claimed they were in the area and had seen what we had seen. And we didn't take that lightly, because we had just experienced a lot of shit we knew these dudes didn't see, and so it escalated fast." Zane didn't want to share the details of this fight in his story, but he shared them with me, and I will tell you this, it got physical. He told me, "We tried to kill them, and we almost did. We sent four of them to the hospital with multiple broken bones." Looking back now, I asked Zane if he regretted his actions that day. He told me he didn't. Which initially caught me off guard, but he went on to explain to me that back then, there was no transition for him from being deployed in a war zone fighting for his life and the lives of his comrades to being back home living in suburbia. He didn't have a light switch in him where he could turn off Zane the Marine Corps sniper fighting for survival and turn on Zane, the twenty-one-year-old young man enjoying sports games and barbecues; or whatever. He told me back then he might as well have been back in Afghanistan fighting, not in a bar in California. He hardly had emotional connections with anyone, which is what he says helped keep him alive when they were deployed. "In the end it shaped us to what we were. You know, one of my biggest mentors in that platoon had been killed, friends had been killed, blown up, had the legs blown off or shot, I'd been blown up, and all this shit had happened, and our contrast of life was so much different. So when I came back to the States, I didn't give a fuck. I was a recluse, and if you weren't my friend, I wanted you to get the fuck out of my face as soon as possible. That was my idea. Obviously now I am way different."

I explained to Zane I somewhat understood, even though I didn't deploy to a hostile environment nor had to worry about my life being taken on a daily basis or see my friends get shot or blown up in front of me, or wonder where my next meal was coming from. But I did experience a somewhat similar situation when I returned from my deployment to GTMO that at least made me able to understand what Zane, and what every military member, experiences when they return from deployments. Being stationed in GTMO was pretty nice. Let's face it, I was stationed on a Caribbean island. But living on an island in the Caribbean for months at a time, you get island fever. And it's not like you are on vacation in the Bahamas, it was work, and I worked in a prison every day. My inmates hated Americans, and they would be sure to let me know. I dealt with a handful who threatened my life and the lives of my family members, but these were idle threats, as I wasn't concerned they'd get out and be able to hunt me down. In fact, I had great rapport and respect with most of them. The poor guards, however, had to deal with riots every day and hunger strikes and suicide attempts. It was pure pandemonium inside the prison back in those days. I had it lucky in the interrogation booths. On the island, you can't drive over 25 mph anywhere. There was one store to shop at, the Navy Exchange, an MWR with pontoon boats, a handful of eateries, two nice gyms, an outdoor movie theater, and you could run; we all took up running the hills. Life was pretty simple; there weren't a lot of choices for anything. You work ten- to fifteen-hour days, go home, run, eat, wake up, and do it again. So when I got back to the States, life seemed complicated, too many choices, and operated way too fast. That was the first time in my life when I was yelling at drivers in my car to slow down. (That lasted about a week.) And all of the worries I left behind, like taking out the trash on time, dealing with the northern Virginia commute with irate drivers, taking the car for oil changes and inspections, stupid everyday bullshit, was there again. And you have to adjust back into that life. I can't imagine what Zane and the rest of the snipers in this book and the rest of the military have to deal with, coming back from a war zone. And we wonder why PTSD exists or why veterans have a hard time communicating with their families again, or finding jobs; it's a tough adjustment, very tough.

Zane told me right after that fight, thankfully, which didn't result in any hardships we'll say, he and his friends all went to the Marine Corps Ball in Las Vegas. "That dude I told you about who told me about Patino dying, he died right after the ball, he flipped his truck. Another good buddy of mine from the CAAT platoon died going to the ball; he was on his motorcycle and got hit by a drunk driver. We had four guys died within weeks after we got back."

GOT BACK AND WENT IN THE BOTTLE

After all this, Zane then went to Sniper School in North Carolina. If you have forgotten, up to now, Zane had been a PIG in a sniper platoon, not a school-trained sniper. After graduating from Scout Sniper School this time in 2011, he went through a Sniper's Leaders course in Camp Pendleton, California, and then he deployed again, back to the same area.

> I was at the same bases a year later. But this time around . . . I wasn't necessarily super-fucking paranoid, but it was the same area that I had been in heavy fighting a year before, so when we were out patrolling, I was thinking, shit is about to pop off! And nothing was going down; no potshots. But there were a ton of IEDs. 3/5 came and ripped us out, then 1/5 ripped them out, and then we ripped 1/5 out in Sangin. So there were all these fucking IEDs everywhere. I was working for weapons company in Wishtan at that time. I engaged a couple targets of opportunity and unfortunately had a good buddy get killed by an IED. A few other buddies got messed up by IEDs, and that's all there was for the most part; IEDs. This deployment was uneventful compared to my last deployment overall. I went from constant firefights daily to none. I had two engagements; that's it. I got back from that deployment and got out of the Marine Corps. And then I went in the bottle for about eight months. I flew out to see my buddies graduate Sniper School and I remember sitting in Sniper School graduation; I had long hair and I was all fucked up. And they were walking across the stage, and I remember seeing how proud they were. Right then, I was like fuck, man, I remember being that proud for doing something. What the fuck have I done? I haven't done shit since I've been out of the Marine Corps. I had been thinking I was doing something, having fun! Partying and shit. I was eating like shit, got overweight, smoking cigarettes like crazy, and drinking my face off every day. Once I saw that, I knew I needed change, so I became a recluse on my ranch for a couple months to get the money to move to North Carolina to where my brother was. All I had was my '46 Chevy.

Zane was twenty-three years old. Realizing that he was letting life drag him down to the bottom of the barrel, more aptly a keg barrel, he decided he had better clean up his act, or his performance would be over. "I called my brother and told him I wanted to move out to North Carolina, and he was like come on, man, so I packed up my truck and went." He arrived in Wilmington, North Carolina, and started to get his life back on track. He is now a private military contractor, and he is deploying again in a month from this interview.

THE WARRIOR SPIRIT

I usually end my interviews by asking the snipers for their parting words on anything they want the readers to know. I didn't even have to ask Zane. He went on talking without missing a beat and told me this:

April 2014 is when the majority of my positive life shifts started happening, mentally and professionally. I had an ex-girlfriend who was very spiritual, and she cracked the door open for me, and then I front-kicked it; I ate it up. I think once I became more conscious and more enlightened, I guess you could say, I was able to one, emotionally release a lot of things, and two, not be regretful or resentful for things that had happened in the past. I became aware that the only things that matter are what is in the present moment, all there is is now, and all there ever will be is now. And whatever has happened to Claudio Patino, Corporal Q (the Marine who was evaporated by the IED), my father, anyone, it didn't matter; I mean, it matters, but it doesn't need to negatively affect me today. And the reason why is because it doesn't exist today. To think about tomorrow all the time, like when we say tomorrow I'll do this, or tomorrow I'll feel better, fuck tomorrow! What if tomorrow never comes? You don't wake up tomorrow and say "It's tomorrow," you wake up and say, "It's today." So I was able to see opportunity, so I could seize opportunities, and I found out what you appreciate, appreciates. So I started diving in head deep. I used to come at the world with closed fists; now I come at it with open arms. I hold two things close to me more than anything in the world. On this path and in my practice I've found that two things drive the warrior spirit, and they are loyalty and integrity: integrity with who and what you are, and being true as fuck with that, and loyalty to what you love. Holding what you love, family and brotherhood, very, very close to you and protecting that with everything that you are. I have this discussion with my blood brother a lot, because we are brothers, best friends, and now we're both combat vets, and have shared a lot of shit together, so it's a very unique relationship. The warrior spirit, or the inner savage, as I like to call it, in us as hyper-masculine males, is unique. I would do anything for my brotherhood, and they would do anything for me, and what we stand for. We believe in this more than anything in the world because it's what connects us to this world more than anything. That is my purpose, to serve my brotherhood and to be loyal to my brotherhood. At the end of the day, hats off to the fucking hitter who's still out there doing it.

AFTERWORD

The Aftermath of a Tactical Decision

MARINES KILL AFGHAN SOLDIERS IN FIREFIGHT WHILE PROTECTING THE U.S. EMBASSY IN KABUL

Here is a story told from a U.S. Marine Corps service member who deployed as a member of Task Force Kabul, an element of the 4th Marine Expeditionary Brigade (Antiterrorism), who has asked to remain anonymous in this publication. He was not a sniper but was intimately familiar with the day-to-day security operations at the U.S. embassy in Kabul, Afghanistan, in 2003, and the members of the Task Force Kabul, which included Marine Corps Scout Snipers. This is neither a success story nor a happy anecdote about beating the enemy and saving lives. It's a story about a tactical decision that was rightly and justly made, but unfortunately cost lives of the innocent. "You can't undo death." They had a split second to make a decision that they will have to live with for the rest of their lives.

TASK FORCE KABUL, U.S. EMBASSY, 2003

The Marine security task forces who were responsible for safeguarding the embassy in Kabul, the capital city of Afghanistan, were on four-month deployment rotations; this story is about the particular task force that had just arrived in Afghanistan at the beginning of May 2003 and were set to return stateside in August. This task force, referred to as Task Force Kabul, was a reinforced company of about 150 to 200 Marines with specialized attachments. Typically, where there is a U.S. embassy in a foreign country, you'll find a Marine Security Guard (MSG) detachment assigned to that embassy, working hand in hand with the embassy's attached Regional Security Office (RSO) and providing security for that embassy; but this wasn't the case in Kabul at the time. The U.S. embassy in Kabul was erected in 1948 but closed its doors in 1989 after the decade-long Soviet-Afghan war, which began in 1979 and ended with the Taliban takeover. When Task Force Kabul took over the embassy, it was nonfunctional.

To give you a better idea of the history of the U.S. embassy in Kabul up to 2003, here is a short timeline of Afghanistan's history with regard to the close political and economic relationship with the Soviet Union and the fighting against mujahideen rebel forces (whom the U.S. assisted at that time, not knowing then we'd be fighting against them beginning in 2001). The timeline was provided by the BBC and is called "Afghan profile— Timeline" (http://www.bbc.com/news/world-south-asia-12024253):

1953—General Mohammed Daud becomes prime minister. Turns to Soviet Union for economic and military assistance. Introduces social reforms, such as abolition of purdah (practice of secluding women from public view).

1963—Mohammed Daud forced to resign as prime minister.

1964—Constitutional monarchy introduced—but leads to political polarisation and power struggles.

1973—Mohammed Daud seizes power in a coup and declares a republic. Tries to play off USSR against Western powers.

1978—General Daud is overthrown and killed in a pro-Soviet coup. The People's Democratic Party comes to power but is paralysed by violent infighting and faces opposition by US-backed mujahideen groups.

Soviet intervention

1979 December—Soviet Army invades and props up communist government.

1980—Babrak Karmal installed as ruler, backed by Soviet troops. But opposition intensifies with various mujahideen groups fighting Soviet forces. US, Pakistan, China, Iran and Saudi Arabia supply money and arms to the mujahideen.

1985—Mujahideen come together in Pakistan to form alliance against Soviet forces. Half of Afghan population now estimated to be displaced by war, with many fleeing to neighbouring Iran or Pakistan.

1986—US begins supplying mujahideen with Stinger missiles, enabling them to shoot down Soviet helicopter gunships. Babrak Karmal replaced by Najibullah as head of Soviet-backed regime.

1988—Afghanistan, USSR, the US and Pakistan sign peace accords and Soviet Union begins pulling out troops.

Red Army quits

1989—Last Soviet troops leave, but civil war continues as mujahideen push to overthrow Najibullah

(In 1989 the U.S. closed the embassy in Kabul. The Soviets had left, and there was no need for the U.S. to be involved with Afghanistan's internal civil war.)

1992—Najibullah's government toppled, but a devastating civil war follows.

1996—Taliban seize control of Kabul and introduce hard-line version of Islam, banning women from work, and introducing Islamic punishments, which include stoning to death and amputations.

1997—Taliban recognised as legitimate rulers by Pakistan and Saudi Arabia. They now control about two-thirds of country.

1998—US launches missile strikes at suspected bases of militant Osama bin Laden, accused of bombing US embassies in Africa.

1999—UN imposes an air embargo and financial sanctions to force Afghanistan to hand over Osama bin Laden for trial.

2001—September—Ahmad Shah Masood, leader of the main opposition to the Taliban—the Northern Alliance—is assassinated.

U.S.-LED INVASION 2001

Of course we know what happened in the U.S. in September 2001. Islamic terrorists attacked our country and killed thousands of Americans. After the 9/11 terrorist attacks and the onset of Operation Enduring

Freedom (OEF), the U.S. invaded Afghanistan to go after the master-mind behind 9/11, Osama bin Laden. When U.S. forces first arrived in Kabul late in 2001, they reopened the doors to the deserted and dilapidated structure and revived the embassy. Although there was no running potable water at that time, the U.S. staffed the building with an RSO, U.S. Aid Office, military elements, and personnel from multiple U.S. agencies. (The embassy has been reconstructed and is fully operational at present.)

In May 2003, Task Force Kabul arrived and took up residency at the embassy, as previous task forces had done as well, and became the embassy's security force (remember, there was no MSG). They worked closely with the Regional Security Officer (RSO) in place at the embassy at that time. (The acronym "RSO" can refer to the office or to the Regional Security Officer.) The officers are special agents from the State Department's Diplomatic Security Service who are responsible for all diplomatic security matters overseas, from threats of terrorist acts to protecting our classified information. They act as security advisors to U.S. ambassadors, and they are also responsible for keeping U.S. personnel and their families stationed overseas safe. They are also the liaison between the host country's law enforcement entities and conduct both criminal and personnel investigations. I don't think any of the Task Force Kabul members during this particular rotation ever thought that in those four months they would become involved in a fatal security incident that would make international headlines, headlines of news stories that would put their own spin on what really happened that day. This story is a firsthand account of that incident, which involved a firefight between U.S. Marines and Afghan soldiers, and the events leading up to the firefight on the May 22, 2003. This story is told not by a sniper, but about a Marine Corps sniper and designated marksmen (DM) and their tactical decisions that resulted in keeping the Embassy safe, but also four dead Afghan National Army (ANA) soldiers.

Before you read the story, however, I'd like to point out the fact that as U.S. citizens, we all have basic constitutional rights: the right to hold property, the right to vote, freedom of speech and religion, etc., and you have the right to draw your own conclusions when you read stories in the media and the right to believe what you read, or not, just as you do reading this story. Most of what we read has the author's spin on it and may have biased information as a result. Even though I am the author of this story and this book, this story, nor any story in this book, is not mine. It is an unbiased firsthand account of a firefight between Marines and Afghan soldiers that unfortunately drew a lot of negative media attention, created political sensitivities, and resulted in tarnished careers. Now that you know that, read this story and formulate your own opinions, but this is what really happened on that day in May 2003.

WEEKS PRIOR TO THE INCIDENT

Let's go back a couple of weeks prior to the incident. While still continuing military operations in Afghanistan under OEF, the U.S. had just begun another campaign in Iraq called Operation Iraqi Freedom (OIF), so the operational tempo was high, and threat conditions were raised all over the globe. Task Force Kabul was established and set in their battle rhythm, a military term used to describe "a deliberate daily cycle of command, staff, and unit activities intended to synchronize current and future operations" (*DoD Dictionary of Military Terms*). They were housed in "modular cans," as they called them, inside the walls of the embassy compound, and worked at the now-operational and staffed embassy building. The embassy compound was located on Great Massoud Road, a four-lane (two eight- to ten-foot-wide lanes going each way), busy, paved throughway, in the Wazir Akbar Khan section of Kabul. The embassy building itself was the main structure in the compound. It was a three-story, aged, concrete structure that wasn't painted but did have air-conditioning and displayed the embassy seal on the front of the building. There were bullet holes in all the windows and plywood nailed up over broken windows. There was a flagpole out in front and a circular driveway. If the embassy came under attack, the personnel working there could either take shelter in the bunker located next to the embassy or in the embassy basement. There were about 250 to 300 Marines living inside the compound during this time.

The compound was surrounded by twelve- to fifteen-foot concrete walls. There were at least four "posts" (think of a watchtower) situated along this wall, all reinforced with sandbags, with additional posts on the roof of the embassy main structure. Post 1 was in front at the main gate to the embassy compound. "The heavier machine guns, like the 240 Gulf supported by the M203 Grenade launcher were used at main gates, not on the posts." Post 2 was also in front of the embassy (this is the post from which the firefight took place). Post 3 was located at the back gate to the compound, and Post 4 was the post on the very top of the embassy roof. "Post 4 was usually manned by snipers, because you could see 360 degrees around the embassy. Since there were not enough snipers in the task force to man the posts 100 percent of the time, they were sometimes manned by infantry Marines and DMs. But there was always either one sniper or one DM on at least one post at all times throughout the twenty-four-hour day."

Snipers, DMs, and infantry are equipped with different weapons and equipment. This may seem obvious to state, but what wasn't immediately obvious at the time was that reports were indicating that the enemy was starting to figure out whether or not the Marine on post was a sniper, DM, or infantry based on what type of weapons and gear they were outfitted with: things like what rifle type they were carrying or whether or not they had binoculars or night vision goggles. "Not only were they able to identify the Marines' MOS (Military Occupational Specialty) essentially, they were able to identify who they were, because they used binoculars to see their nametapes on their uniforms." When Task Force Kabul began to realize the enemy was collecting this information on them, they quickly changed practices, and nametapes came off for operational security. Why would the enemy care whether or not the Marine was a sniper? Because snipers had bounties on their heads, and if you are targeting the enemy, you want to take out their most efficient weapons system, in this case a highly trained Marine Corps sniper.

Behind the embassy was in a local Afghan neighborhood, the International Security Assistance Force (ISAF) headquarters was located close by down the street, and the Afghan National Army (ANA) and the Afghan National Intelligence (ANI) Service were located directly across the street. The ISAF was a NATO-led security mission to help restore the Afghanistan government and keep Afghanistan safe from insurgent groups, specifically the Taliban and al-Qaeda.

The environment and atmosphere in Kabul at that time was what you would think of when you picture a third-world country: habitable living conditions, but polluted and completely unsanitary. When you are an

Armed Forces member in any service and you deploy, as soon as you set foot on the ground, or deck, on your deployment, you get the mandatory "in-country prebrief," as you have read in some of the sniper stories already. It covers safety issues, liberty (if you get that), general orders, and so on—basically what you need to do to stay safe and out of trouble. So during Task Force Kabul's prebrief, they were told that 70 percent of the air in Kabul was filled with fecal matter. There is no sanitization, no sewer systems, no trash pickup, and no flushable toilets. "I saw a kid, he was about twelve years old, on the sidewalk, lift up his man dress and take a shit right there on the side of the street in front of everyone." Whatever waste there was—human waste, garbage, materials—was burned inside the city proper. That was the air quality that was circulating in their lungs for four months. "It was very hot, dusty, and the water in the rivers always seemed to be low. I can't remember it raining. They said in the winter when the snow melts in the mountains, the rivers would fill up." Aside from the wells dug by U.S. aid organizations, there was no potable water. Pallets of water were shipped in from the U.S. that equaled the size of a football field so the U.S. personnel could drink it and brush their teeth. "Everything was blown to shit, buildings, palaces, from us and from the Russians. It looked like a true war zone. We would weapons train in the mountains, and all these little kids would come out of the woodwork to collect our brass. They never had any shoes on, and there were no adults anywhere to be found." As the U.S. presence increased, however, so did small commerce. Businesses sprung up that sold, bartered, or traded goods. "You could find anything on Chicken Street: porcelain objects, carpets, antique weapons, linen. Vendors would sell things that you had no idea how these items made it to Afghanistan and on Chicken Street. Deep in Kabul you had the electronics black market sector; it reminded me of a mall in the early 1980s."

Even though the living conditions, according to our standards, were inhospitable, the Afghans were not. "You couldn't walk by an Afghan house without being invited in for tea or whatever. What little they had they shared; that is their culture. They went out of their way to be hospitable."

Now that you have a mental picture of the environment around the U.S. embassy in Kabul at that time, let's get to the events that led up to the controversial, fatal firefight. The ANA compound was a long, rectangular two-story building, located directly across the street from the embassy and walled in like the embassy, "but their walls were constructed of more man-made materials; they weren't reinforced concrete like these walls. There were no posts, or watchtowers, around the wall, but there was a soldier at the main gate that faced the road who sat off to the side in a chair when the gate was open. Although it was the ANA building, ANI was co-located in that building as well."

Factors such as the ANA/ANI being located in very close proximity to the U.S. embassy, the heightened security at the time (worldwide due to terror attacks), the tensions from the U.S. presence in the Middle East, and the almost lackadaisical behavior of the ANA/ANI soldiers with regard to security, resulted in more than one occasion when high-level embassy officials directed the RSO to walk across the street to liaise with the ANA regarding security matters. One such incident happened a few weeks prior to the firefight. The ambassador got tired of looking at the turret of the gun mounted on an old, broken-down BMP (*Boyevaya Mashina Pekhoty*, a Soviet infantry fighting vehicle) that the ANA had parked inside their compound, which was pointed directly at the embassy. He sent the RSO over to ask the ANA if they could swing the gun turret around and point it in another direction. His staff was not comfortable working in a building that had a BMP gun turret aimed at it. It also sent the wrong signal to other coalition forces in the area who could observe the ANA in effect "targeting" the embassy. The ambassador was pretty sure it was a benign occurrence, but nonetheless, he wanted it moved.

The RSO complied and went over to talk to the ANA. After a few failed attempts to have the ANA reposition their BMP turret, the deputy RSO, along with other members of the task force, decided to take a "delegation" over to visit the ANA leadership, intent on not leaving until the ANA adjusted the BMP turret. The personal delegation visit proved successful: the ANA finally moved the BMP turret away from the U.S. embassy. After doing so, the Afghans told them the only reason they kept the BMP turret pointed toward the embassy was merely as a means of getting the Marines to come over and have tea with them. Although amused, the task force delegation told the ANA that pointing a gun at them wasn't the best course of action to coax them over. They politely explained to the ANA that they had to take security violations a bit more seriously while in their country. It didn't mean they couldn't be friendly, but they had to maintain their security posture. There was no harm done, the issue was solved, and the ambassador and embassy staff relaxed and went back to work.

The day before the firefight, another situation occurred in which the ANA did something that made the U.S. second-guess their true intentions; were they really the friendly neighbors across the street who used guns to lure them over for tea, or were there a few bad apples in the bunch? It was May 21, and a Marine was manning Post 2. He observed an event that met the rules of engagement (ROE) at that time, one of which was, if a weapon was pointed at U.S. forces, that was grounds for the use of deadly force—basically fire at whatever or whoever was aiming at them. Now, Marines are trained and experienced to assess and analyze a situation before pulling the trigger; you have already read about the significance this has in some of the previous stories. You also know that the ANA had already violated the ROE essentially by aiming their BMP turret at the embassy; but after being asked politely to move it, they complied and resolved the situation. But they still either wittingly or unwittingly violated the ROE. So on this day the Marine on Post 2 watched as either an ANI or ANA soldier tossed what appeared to be the body of a grenade at the base of the wall right below his post. Although the immediate reaction to this show of force would be to shoot, the Marine didn't shoot. Because of his training and keen observation skills, he was able to see that the grenade was not a live grenade; it was a training grenade. A training grenade is usually a different shape and color, and it is hollow with a big hole through the center; a real grenade is solid and heavy with no hole. The Marine reported the event to the deputy RSO, who went to investigate the scene, and sure enough, he walked out to the wall, found the grenade, and confirmed that it was indeed a training grenade. Perplexed, and a bit aggravated, he went to visit the ANA leadership, again. And again he had to explain to the ANA that his Marines were highly trained to be reactionary to any possible threats or acts of violence toward the Embassy, and they weren't to be taken lightheartedly. Think of police dogs, K9s; they are highly trained, reactionary dogs that are with their handler to do a specific job. They are not there to be petted and cuddled like a house pet, and we know this; so we don't go over to them, even with good intentions, and pet their heads, because they may take our hands off. This is the same relation-ship. "You don't pet a rattlesnake; you don't point a gun at the U.S. em-bassy that has U.S. Marines guarding it, nor do you haphazardly throw a grenade, trainer or not, at the wall beneath their posts. If you do, you are asking for trouble." Whether you want to call it the unspoken rules, etiquette, or protocol of war, you know what you shouldn't do to avoid provoking a negative response. The task force Marines on post were on alert at all times; they are the K9s and the rattlesnakes that shouldn't be messed with, because they have a job to do, and that's the only thing they are there to do. Thankfully, though, in both situations the Marines' observation and analytical thinking let them conduct a quick assessment before being reactionary and pulling their triggers. Up to this point, the ANA had a gun turret aimed at the embassy, and now an ANA soldier flippantly threw a grenade, albeit a training grenade, at the embassy wall. And if you look at the pictures, you can see that the ANA soldier didn't just drop a grenade on the ground outside the embassy wall; he had to throw it across that four-lane street to hit the embassy wall. Now why would he do that?

So the question became, were the ANA that oblivious to their actions, or were they taunting and testing the embassy security? The RSO told the ANA leadership that this behavior was unacceptable, and should another similar incident arise, the Marines might take action in response to negligent movements by the ANA soldiers and engage them with fire. To avoid this unnecessary action, the RSO wanted to ensure the ANA knew not to provoke his Marine security force anymore, because they were trained to engage if they felt the embassy security was threatened in any way. The ANA respectfully stated that they clearly understood and would take care of the problem to make sure it didn't happen again. The last thing the RSO, ambassador and U.S. needed was to have an international incident due to negligence; unfortunately, though, that's exactly what they got.

THE INCIDENT

"May 22, 2003, started off to be a good morning; the weather was pleas-ant, and there were no security issues the previous night, giving the

Monday morning an overall sense of calmness." At approximately 0800 hours a task force convoy to Bagram Air Base (BAB) departed from the embassy with a quarter of the task force combat power, which was approximately forty to fifty people. This was a standard-size force for a convoy mission due to the distance and nature of the route to BAB. After the convoy departed, somewhere between 1000 and 1015 hours, a vehicle pulled up to the ANA/ANI side of the street across from Post 2 at the U.S. embassy. From Post 1 and Post 2, it appeared to the Marine snipers and DMs manning the posts that ANA soldiers were unloading AK-47s and carrying them into the compound. The Marines watched the activity without trepidation, because their initial assessment was that it was a nonthreatening, simple logistical event. It wasn't until one specific and deliberate action occurred that that unassuming day turned into a bloody battle.

There were about five to eight ANA soldiers unloading small-arms weapons from the truck; mostly AK-47s. One of the ANA soldiers decided to once again test the resolve of the embassy security; or was it a test? He grabbed one of the rifles they were unloading, swung it around to face the embassy, shouldered it, and aimed it directly at the Marines standing watch on Post 2. At that instant the Marines on Post 2 had a weapon pointing directly at them. This was not a case of an unmanned ANA BMP with the turret pointing at the embassy, or an ANA soldier flippantly throwing a training grenade at the embassy wall; this time an ANA soldier purposely turned around to aim a rifle directly at the Marines in Post 2. If you were a Marine sniper looking through your scope into the barrel of a rifle pointed at you, what would you do? Well, this Marine's training kicked in, and he fired at the ANA soldier. The ANA soldier took a shot directly to the head. As the Marine sniper fired, the other Marines on the embassy rooftop posts began engaging the targets below almost simultaneously with their M40 sniper rifles, while the task force Marines on Post 1 opened up with an M240G machine gun. In response to the Marine firepower, the ANA attempted to fire back, hitting the glass of the embassy building to include the U.S. ambassador's window. In a matter of minutes, approximately three ANA soldiers were dead and several injured. After seven minutes, the deputy task force commander yelled ceasefire from the wall of Post 2 and then called it over the radios. During this short, but deadly, firefight, the embassy went into lockdown and all task force Marines were 100 percent manned, meaning every task force Marine was in or on his way to a preplanned fighting positions. The incident spread like wildfire, and other U.S. forces and U.S. bases in the region immediately raised their threat condition and went to a heightened state of combat readiness. Even the task force convoy that had departed earlier that morning was on lockdown at BAB. The task force convoy commander had to speak directly to the BAB general to convince him to allow the convoy, which remember had a quarter of task force Kabul's combat power, to return to the embassy to assist with providing security so the embassy could have its full complement of security forces in place.

THE AFTERMATH

After the ceasefire, the task force commander had to immediately look into the details of the firefight and report the details from everybody who was involved to the ambassador, the RSO, and higher local and stateside headquarters personnel. The bloody aftermath revealed that three ANA soldiers were killed; one from a head shot from the rooftop post, one from the M240G machine gun on Post 1, and one from a rifle shot from Post 2.

A full U.S.-led investigation was conducted. For over three weeks investigators were at the U.S. embassy questioning and interviewing the Task Force Kabul members and eyewitnesses. In conclusion, no Task Force Kabul Marine was found at fault in their actions taken to protect the embassy and its personnel inside. The U.S. ambassador fully supported the Marines' actions and their reason for engagement. "The task force commander did, however, receive a soft relief; for political purposes in my view. That day reinforced a saying I reiterate in my mind: 'what we do in life, echoes in eternity.'" The split-second choice made that day by those Marines trained to defend the embassy against threats had lifelong repercussions. For some it was the relief of duty and a negative mark on their service record, which could affect them the next time they came around for promotion. For others it was the act of killing another human, not knowing 100 percent if they had intent to kill him first, even though their posture said they did. And for others, it was the relief that the Marines were as highly trained as they were and because of that, there was a chance to return home safely and unharmed. The embassy remained secure, and the Marines returned to business as usual. Several weeks later, relations with the ANA returned to normal. They were very regretful for the incident, and the Task Force Kabul members expressed their empathy for the unnecessary loss of life.

The press had a field day with this story, as you can imagine. The *New York Times* wrote an article on the incident and published it on May 22, 2003, titled "AFTEREFFECTS: KABUL; Marines at U.S. Embassy Kill 3 Afghan Soldiers in Incident Called Error" (http://www.nytimes .com/2003/05/22/world/aftereffects-kabul-marines-us-embassy-kill -3-afghan-soldiers-incident-called.html). The article stated, "Afghan officials said they accepted the explanation that the shooting was a mistake and that the American soldiers had found the Afghans' actions suspicious." The article interviewed the cousin of one of the wounded Afghan soldiers, who said this: "'What we want to know is why they started this,' said Daulat Khan, 33, whose cousin was among those injured. Afghan troops have occupied the base opposite the American Embassy for a year and a half since taking control of Kabul city, he said. 'Those people who started the shooting should be brought to justice,' he said."

Reuters published an article as well, titled "U.S. soldiers mistakenly kill four Afghans" (http://www.afghanistannewscenter.com/news/2003/ may/may222003.html). This article states, "U.S. troops have shot dead four Afghan soldiers and wounded four others outside the U.S. embassy in Kabul when they mistakenly thought they were about to come under attack, Afghan officials say." And then you read, "Another intelligence official added: 'The U.S. soldiers thought the Afghan soldiers were aiming guns at them. They panicked and opened fire.'" But now you know, from a firsthand account, that the Afghan soldier did indeed shoulder and aim a rifle directly at the Marines on Post 2, after the two earlier incidents where the ANA compromised the U.S. embassy's security. The ANA were repeatedly and politely told not to provoke the U.S. security forces at the embassy. The ANA stated that they understood. Perhaps the ANA leadership didn't pass that word to all of the ANA soldiers. Who knows? Did the Marines on post that day panic, or just do their job? The Marines confirmed that an AK-47 was aimed at them; what they couldn't confirm is whether or not the Afghan aiming the

AK-47 was going to follow through and fire the weapon. They can't read minds—no one can; they read actions and movement, and the movement said, "I'm going to shoot this gun at you."

A story by Paul Wolf published on May 28, 2003, called "Lockdown at U.S. Embassy in Kabul" (http://www.ratical.org/ratville/CAH/USE lockdown.html), states this: "A week ago Wednesday, May 21, 2003, US troops shot to death four Afghan soldiers in front of the US embassy in Kabul. The Afghans were being trained by the International Security Assistance Forces (ISAF) guarding the city, comprised of German, French, and others, located right across the street. The Afghan soldiers were in uniform and carrying weapons, and the US troops apparently mistook them for enemy combatants. For the next five days, angry Afghans held a protest in front of the US embassy, at the site of the killings." After reading this, you think the Marines thought the Afghan soldiers, who were being trained by ISAF, *who were on our side,* were enemy combatants, not the Afghan soldiers from across the street; the same soldiers who initiated the two previous incidents against the U.S. embassy security. In Mr. Wolf's words, "By the time I arrived to photograph the five day old protest, which was yesterday, the entire block around the embassy had been closed off by the police, and the protest was no more." And then he goes on to say, "The trip wasn't entirely a waste, though, as I did gain some insight as to how the US soldiers think. One PAO warned me of the dangers of Afghanistan and its people. 'More than half' of them, I was told, were highly dangerous, just waiting for an opportunity to strike. I was told not to carry money, or my passport, or talk to strangers, etc. This attitude, plus the unreported death of a US soldier last week—shot by a sniper on the same road from Jalalabad I had traveled a few days later—helps explain why the US troops killed the Afghan soldiers in front of the embassy." According to Mr. Wolf, the Marines fired at the Afghan soldier because they thought every Afghan was highly dangerous and because a U.S. soldier was shot the week prior. Not, however, and I stress this, because an ANA soldier aimed a rifle directly at the Marines on Post 2. They were in Afghanistan, tensions were high, and Marines were there to protect the embassy and not to liaise with host country nationals. That is someone else's job, so if someone or something threatened them, they would take out the threat; that was their job.

We are lucky that we have freedom of speech. However, knowing that should make us cautious when deciding what to believe in the news. People are entitled to their opinions, and as I've stated before, will write with biases and judgments and take sides. You may even think I am writing with one here, taking the side of the Marines. My intentions are only to show you how three different articles on the same incident make claims and accusations as to why the Marines shot the Afghan soldiers, and then to provide you with a firsthand account of the events that day.

The stress and anxiety in situations like this come from ensuring that service members are executing their mission and ensuring that we do everything in our power to limit U.S. casualties and unnecessary loss of life. An event like this happens so quickly that your instincts and training take over and you immediately take action in a cohesive and collective manner.

We all can *what-if* a situation and backseat quarterback it for days, months, and maybe even longer. But the reality is, those Marines were trained to respond to that situation, which is why they go through rigorous training: to be able to make decisions that will ultimately impact a lot of people in some way, and to be able to handle that decision and its consequences emotionally later on. Unless we were in their shoes, had the training and responsibility of protecting that embassy, unless we had a foreign national pointing a rifle at us, knowing the political sensitivities at that time, then we shouldn't second-guess their decisions; we aren't trained or qualified to.

It's understandable, after reading these articles, why we might ask ourselves, "Why did the Marines shoot at the Afghan soldiers who were not anti-American, who once fought beside Americans, and who were peacefully co-located alongside Americans on the same street?" Or, "The Marines must have known the ANA soldiers were negligent, so why didn't they wait to shoot?" But now let's look at it from another standpoint: let's say the Marines did wait to see what that Afghan soldier intended to do and didn't fire immediately, and as a result, they took a shot in the head from the Afghan soldier. What if the other Afghan soldiers grabbed the weapons they were loading and opened fire on the embassy? Then we would be reading this article asking ourselves, "Why didn't the Marines shoot him? That Afghan soldier pointed a rifle directly at them, which met their rules of engagement to fire?"

Adding to the delusion of the reported incident, the press doesn't mention that this was the third incident in which the ANA had threatened the security of the U.S. embassy. Could the Afghans have been that naive all three times? Or were they probing and testing the Marines to see how they responded to prepare for the real attack? The answer is, we'll never know. And unfortunately, with the press, it's now become a case of he said, she said.

We don't know what we don't know. But now you do know the behind-the-scenes of this story, even though it's dated. You may now understand and have a better appreciation for why military members may seem tight-lipped when it comes to reporters and to being interviewed. It's very unfortunate that our military members have to endure this pressure alongside the normal pressures and stress of just being in the military and deployed in a hostile environment on foreign land away from their families. And for those of you who think, "They signed up for it, so I don't sympathize with them"; well, you should also know that for those who did voluntarily sign up, it might have been their only option left before having to live on the streets. Not everyone who joins the military does so as a patriotic duty to serve their nation, or to go to be a GI Joe or GI Jane. Many individuals join the military so they have a shot at earning a clean, respectable living, and many do it because they have no other choice. I commend this, because it's a heck of a lot easier to steal, sell drugs, join gangs, and live the life of a criminal than to challenge yourself and push your limits both mentally and physically to be successful. I personally know the person who shared this story with me, and if he hadn't joined the Marines on his own initiative, he might have met the same untimely, sad fate his father did, and that was being gunned down by gang members before the age of thirty.

You have read many stories from and about Marine Corps Scout Snipers in this book. You've read the common threads woven throughout them all; the arduous training, the sadness of leaving behind families, the shock of combat and near-death experiences, the pain of watching their brothers die before them, and having to live with the consequences of choices and decisions they've made as Scout Snipers. And although they all have experienced these emotions at one point or another in their careers as Snipers, they all told me they couldn't have been more proud to be one.

GLOSSARY OF MILITARY ACRONYMS, TERMS, SLANG, WEAPONS, AND DEFINITIONS

0351—Military Occupational Specialty in the United States Marine Corps for Infantry Assaultman.

1/5—The unit designator for 1st Battalion, 5th Marine Regiment, written as 1/5. The 1st Battalion falls under the command of the 5th Marine Regiment, which falls under command of the 1st Marine Division (MARDIV). 1/5 is a United States Marine Corps infantry battalion based out of Marine Corps Base Camp Pendleton in California. The battalion was formed in 1914 and has served in many major conflicts since then, including the Global War on Terror (GWOT).

120mm Smoothbore Cannon—The 120mm ammunition system equips the M1E1 (Abrams) tank with a 120mm main armament. It consists of a family of kinetic energy (KE) rounds and a family of high explosive antitank (HEAT) rounds. The 120mm smoothbore cannon system was developed by West Germany for the Leopard II tank. The ammunition produced by both countries is interoperable and interchangeable between the Abrams and the Leopard, thus ensuring maximum commonality within the NATO community (https://fas.org/man/dod-101/sys/land/120.htm).

11—Refers to one of the core Marine Corps infantry MOS's, 0311, rifleman. Some people will call 0311s "11s."

2/4—The unit designator for 2nd Battalion, 4th Marines, written as 2/4. The 2nd Battalion falls under the command of the 4th Marines and is part of the 5th Marine Regiment, which falls under command of the 1st MARDIV. 2/4 is a United States Marine Corps infantry battalion based out of Marine Corps Base Camp Pendleton in California. 2/4 was constituted in April 1914 during World War I, when it was activated as one of the three battalions of the 4th Marine Regiment. The battalion has served in many major conflicts since then, including GWOT.

2/5—The unit designator for 2nd Battalion, 5th Marine Regiment, written as 2/5. The 2nd Battalion falls under the command of the 5th Marine Regiment, which falls under command of the 1st MARDIV. 2/5 is a United States Marine Corps infantry battalion based out of Marine Corps Base Camp Pendleton in California. The battalion was formed in 1914 and has served in many major conflicts since then, including GWOT.

2/8—The unit designator for 2nd Battalion, 8th Marine Regiment, written as 2/8. The 2nd Battalion falls under the command of the 8th Marine Regiment, which falls under command of the 2nd MARDIV. 2/8 is a United States Marine Corps infantry battalion based out of Marine Corps Base Camp Lejeune, North Carolina. 2/8 was activated in 1940 and has served in many major conflicts since then, including GWOT.

3/6—The unit designator for 3rd Battalion, 6th Marine Regiment, written as 3/6. The 3rd Battalion falls under the command of the 6th Marine Regiment, which falls under command of the 2nd MARDIV. 3/6 is a United States Marine Corps infantry battalion based out of Marine Corps Base Camp Lejeune, North Carolina. 3/6 was activated in 1917. Battalion Landing Team is a subordinate unit. 3/6 has served in many major conflicts since WWI to present-day GWOT.

3/7—The unit designator for 3rd Battalion, 7th Marine Regiment, written as 3/7. The 3rd Battalion falls under the command of the 7th Marine Regiment, which falls under command of the 1st MARDIV. 3/7 is a United States Marine Corps infantry battalion based out of Marine Corps Air Ground Combat Center (MCAGCC) in Twentynine Palms, California. 3/7 was activated January 1, 1941, at Guantanamo Bay, Cuba, and was assigned to the 1st Marine Brigade. In February

1941 they were reassigned to the 1st Marine Division. The battalion has been in combat since WWII to present-day GWOT.

31—Refers to the Marine Corps Military Occupational Specialty 0331, machine gunner.

556—Refers to 5.56mm small-caliber rifle cartridge.

A10—Refers to the A10 Thunderbolt, also known by its nicknames, "Warthog" and "Hog". It's a fixed-wing fighter jet used for close air support (CAS). Its secondary mission is to provide airborne forward air control (FAC), directing other aircraft in attacks on ground targets (https://en.wikipedia.org/wiki/Fairchild_Republic_A-10_Thunderbolt_II).

AAR—An acronym that stands for After Action Report.

AAV—An acronym that stands for Assault Amphibious Vehicle. Marines refer to them as "amtracks," short for their original designation, "amphibious tractor."

AC-130—Refers to Lockheed's AC-130 gunship, a heavily armed ground-attack aircraft solely for use by the United States Air Force.

ADSW—An acronym that stands for Active Duty for Special Work.

AK-47—Refers to the Soviet 7.62mm assault rifle officially known as the *Avtomat Kalashnikova*, or just Kalashnikova, often pronounced as "kalishnakoff."

Ammo—Short for "ammunition."

Amtrack—Short for "amphibious tractor," now called assault amphibious vehicles.

ANA—Refers to the Afghan National Army.

ANI—Refers to the Afghan National Intelligence.

ARS—An acronym that stands for Amphibious Reconnaissance School.

ATIC—An acronym that stands for Advanced Targeting Intelligence Cell.

BAB—Refers to Bagram Air Base in Bagram, Afghanistan.

Battle Rhythm—Refers to the military term used to describe "a deliberate daily cycle of command, staff, and unit activities intended to synchronize current and future operations" (*DoD Dictionary of Military Terms*).

Billet—A military term for a specific personnel position, assignment, or duty station, as well as living (or "berthing," a term used in the United States Navy) quarters.

Blue on Blue—A military term that refers to friendly forces accidentally targeting and killing other friendly forces during combat.

BMP—Refers to the *Boyevaya Mashina Pekhoty*, a Soviet infantry fighting vehicle.

Boot PIG—Refers to a slang term used by Marines to signify a "boot," meaning junior, and PIG, meaning a Professionally Instructed Gunman, not yet a graduate of Scout Sniper School.

BUD/S—An acronym that stands for Basic Underwater Demolition/SEAL School, often called "buds."

CAAT—An acronym that stands for Combined Anti-Armor Team.

CAGS—An acronym that stands for Combined Armed Exercise.

Camo—A term used for "camouflaged."

CAS—An acronym that stands for Close Air Support.

CASEVAC—An acronym that stands for Casualty Evacuations.

Chow Hall—A term used in the military to refer to a dining area or cafeteria on a military installation. On a Navy ship it's called a "mess deck."

CI—An acronym that stands for Counterintelligence.

Civvies—Slang term that refers to civilian clothes.

COA—An acronym that stands for Course of Action.

Cobra—Refers to the Bell AH-1 Cobra, a single-engine attack helicopter manufactured by Bell Helicopter.

COC—An acronym that stands for Command Operations Center, pronounced as "see-o-see." COC can also refer to a Combat Operations Center.

COG—An acronym that stands for Corporals of the Guard. Smaller-size rotating groups of post standers and their supervisor are referred to as the Corporals of the Guard. The "COG" specifically refers to the leader or supervisor of the group of post standers, which is normally the rank of corporal in the Marine Corps.

Comms—Short for "communications."

CONUS—An acronym that stands for Continental United States.

Corpsman—An enlisted medical specialist in the United States Navy who serves with both the Navy and the Marine Corps.

CQB—An acronym that stands for Close Quarters Battle. CQB is close-range fighting where individuals engage the enemy with personal weapons. It could potentially end up to where individuals have to engage in hand-to-hand combat. CQB is used when tactically entering and clearing buildings in a hostile environment.

CRE—An acronym that stands for Commanders Readiness Evaluation.

DM—An acronym that stands for Designated Marksman.

DMR—An acronym that stands for Designated Marksman Rifle.

DOPE—An acronym that stands for Data on Previous Engagement. DOPE is the information snipers enter in a log that includes details of particular shots they've taken to include things like rifle and ammunition performance, temperature, wind speed, altitude, etc., so that if the same conditions exist again, the sniper can use the recorded data to assist him in making an accurate shot.

FAC—An acronym that stands for Forward Air Control. FAC is the provisional guidance to CAS making sure an aircraft hits its intended target without injury to friendly troops.

FAP—An acronym that stands for Fleet Assistance Program. According to the MARINE CORPS ORDER 1000.8, "The FAP is a method by which the tenant Fleet Marine Force (FMF) commanders and the host supporting installation commander agree to personnel requirements beyond the personnel capabilities of the host command. It is intended to provide the host command with sufficient manpower resources to accomplish current, new, or increased workload to support the tenant FMF commands. The agreement will stipulate those host manpower requirements that will be borne by the tenant FMF commands. The primary objective of the FAP is to augment the manpower resources of the host activity so that it may provide adequate support to its tenant FMF units without degrading the FMF's combat readiness. A secondary objective of the FAP is to provide enhanced opportunities for FMF Marines whose MOS could be put to better use in a garrison situation by the host commander."

FAST—An acronym that stands for Fleet Antiterrorism Security Team.

FITREP—An acronym that stands for Fitness Report. It is an evaluation report used in the U.S. Navy and the U.S. Marine Corps. In the U.S. Navy, Navy chief petty officers (E-7 to E-9) and officers are given Fitness Reports, while Navy enlisted members E-6 and below are issued Evaluation Reports, referred to as "EVALs." Marine enlisted personnel from the rank of sergeant (E-5) to sergeant major or master gunnery sergeant (E-9) and officers are given FITREPs, while junior Marines are given Proficiency and Conduct marks, referred to as "Pros/Cons."

Flak Jacket—Refers to protective body armor worn like a vest that has plates inside. Flak jackets were originally designed to protect against shrapnel only but today can protect against bullets as well. The word "flak" is a contraction for German *Flugzeugabwehrkanone* (which translates to mean anti-aircraft cannon).

FLOT—An acronym that stands for Forward Line of Troops.

FO—An acronym that stands for Forward Observer.

FOB—An acronym that stands for Forward Operating Base.

Ghillie Suit—A ghillie suit is a personnel concealment suit. It is camouflaged clothing that is meant to resemble foliage. It allows a person to blend into the natural landscape by breaking up the outline of the person wearing it. The suits will actually move in the wind just like the surrounding foliage. One tends to look like Big Foot when wearing it. There are different types, but usually you can get them in the form of a jacket and pants suit or a type of poncho suit.

GOSP—An acronym that stands for Gas-Oil Separation Plant.

GRG—An acronym that stands for Gridded Reference Graphic.

Grunt—The term "grunt" refers to a military member who's in the infantry. In the Marine Corps that is anyone whose Military Occupational Specialty (MOS) is preceded by the number 03. For example, the MOS 0311—Basic Rifleman is a grunt, infantry, and rifleman.

GTMO—An acronym that stands for "Guantanamo," referring to Guantanamo Bay in Cuba.

Gunner—A term used in the Marine Corps that refers to Marines with the MOS 0306, infantry weapons officers, who are commonly referred to as "gunner" or "Marine gunner." Gunners are nontechnical chief warrant officers (CWO2 to CWO5) that are weapons specialists.

Gunny—Short for gunnery sergeant, the seventh enlisted rank in the United States Marine Corps.

Helo—Short for helicopter.

HIMARS—An acronym that stands for High Mobility Artillery Rocket System. According to Army-Technology.com (http://www.army-technology.com/projects/himars/), HIMARS was developed by Lockheed Martin Missiles and Fire Control under an advanced concept technology demonstration (ACTD) program, placed in 1996. The purpose of HIMARS is to engage and defeat artillery, air defense concentrations, trucks, light armor and personnel carriers, as well as support troop and supply concentrations. HIMARS launches its weapons and moves away from the area at high speed before enemy forces locate the launch site.

HOG—An acronym that stands for Hunters of Gunmen; Marine Corps school–trained Scout Snipers.

HOGs Tooth—A HOGs tooth is what you get when you graduate the Marine Corps Scout Sniper Basic Course (SSBC). It's a 762 bullet that hangs from 550 cord, an all-purpose cord.

HMMWV—An acronym that stands for High Mobility Multipurpose Wheeled Vehicle (HMMWV), commonly known as and called Humvee.

HRST—An acronym that stands for Helicopter Rope Suspension Training.

IED—An acronym that stands for Improvised Explosive Device.

IED Daisy Chain—Refers to multiple IEDs rigged together in a sequence or ring.

INDOC—A term that stands for "indoctrination." It is common slang in the military. For Marine Corps Infantry wanting to become snipers, indoc refers to the two-week school they go through, which is very rigorous training, not a classroom environment. It is not a gentleman's course. They are screened by the snipers in the STA Platoon to see if they have what it takes to make it in Scout Sniper Basic Course (SSBC).

IR Panel—Refers to an infrared signaling device that alerts other friendly forces in the area of your location so there are no "blue on blue" casualties.

ISAF—An acronym that stands for International Security Assistance Force.

ISR—An acronym that stands for Infantry Squad Radio.

ITG—An acronym that stands for Infrared Trail Guide.

JTAC—An acronym that stands for Joint Terminal Attack Controller and is the term used in the United States Armed Forces for a qualified military service member who, from a forward position, directs the action of combat aircraft engaged in close air support and other

offensive air operations (http://www.military.com/video/operations
-and-strategy/air-strikes/jtac-calling-in-air-strikes/2484564598001).

LAV—An acronym that stands for Light Armored Vehicle.

Libo—A military term that is short for "liberty," which refers to when a
military member is on leave: has time off from his/her duty.

LOA—An acronym that stands for Limit of Advance. The LOA is a
designated area, an easily recognized terrain feature, beyond which
attacking elements will not advance.

LOD—An acronym that stands for Line of Departure, the line designated to attack enemy forces from.

LSD-42—LSD refers to a dock landing ship in the U.S. Navy. LSDs support amphibious operations. LSD-42 refers to the USS Germantown.

M203—A grenade launcher that is attached to an M16 or M4 rifle under the barrel and fires a 40mm grenade.

M240G—A medium machine gun mounted on vehicles, aircraft, and
watercraft and carried by the infantry.

M4—The M4 carbine is a shorter and lighter variant of the M16A2 assault rifle.

M40—A bolt-action sniper rifle. Variations include the M40A1 and
M40A3. The M40A3 is the .50 caliber variation.

M49—A spotting scope also known as the M49 observation telescope. It
is a multipurpose scope system used primarily for long-range marksmanship observation.

MAGTF—An acronym that stands for Marine Air Ground Task Force.
It's a United States Marine Corps term to describe the principal organization for all missions across the range of military operations in
the Marine Corps. According to the official website of the USMC,
"MAGTFs are a balanced air-ground, combined arms task organization
of Marine Corps forces under a single commander that is structured
to accomplish a specific mission. The MAGTF was formalized by the
publishing of Marine Corps Order 3120.3 in December of 1963."

Mark 11 (MK11)—The United States Marine Corps Sniper Weapon
System (SWS) based on the SR-25 (Stoner 7.62mm automatic rifle).

MARSOC—An acronym that stands for Marine Corps Forces Special
Operations Command.

MCRD—An acronym that stands for Marine Corps Recruit Depot.
MCRDs are where all new Marines go through their initial training,

commonly referred to as "boot camp," a thirteen-week training program that they must complete in order to serve in the United States Marine Corps.

MEB(AT)—An acronym that stands for Marine Expeditionary Brigade (MEB) Antiterrorism (AT).

Medevac—A term for medical evacuation, sometimes written as "medivac."

MEU—An acronym that stands for Marine Expeditionary Unit.

MOPP Gear—MOPP is an acronym that stands for Mission Oriented Protective Posture. MOPP gear is protective gear, to include things like masks, gloves, garment coverings and boot coverings, worn in a toxic environment such as during a chemical, biological, radiological, or nuclear (CBRN) strike.

MOS—An acronym that stands for Military Occupational Specialty.

MOUT—An acronym that stands for Military Operations in Urban Terrain.

MP—An acronym that stands for Military Police.

MRE—An acronym that stands for Meal Ready-to-Eat.

MSG—An acronym that stands for Marine Security Guard.

MTT—An acronym that stands for Military Transition Team.

Muj—Pronounced *mooj*, it's a slang term that is short for mujahideen. Mujahideen is plural for mujahid, which is Arabic for one engaged in jihad. Mujahideen loosely refers to any type of insurgent, guerrilla, or Islamic extremist.

NAM—An acronym that stands for Navy and Marine Corps Achievement Medal. A NAM with a *V* (the *V* device is a miniature bronze or gold letter *V*, which stands for combat valor).

NCIS—An acronym that stands for Naval Criminal Investigative Service.

NCO—An acronym that stands for Noncommissioned Officers.

NJP—An acronym that stands for Nonjudicial Punishment in the U.S. Armed Forces.

NVG—An acronym that stands for Night Vision Goggles.

OCONUS—An acronym that stands for Outside the Continental United States.

OCS—An acronym that stands for U.S. Marine Corps Officer Candidate School and The Basic School (OCS/TBS).

OEF—An acronym that stands for Operation Enduring Freedom.

Officer Country—A military term when on a U.S. Navy ship that refers to where the officer quarters are located, which is designated by the blue tile on the floor.

OIF—An acronym that stands for Operation Iraqi Freedom.

OPLAN—An acronym that stands for Operational Plans.

Overwatch—Is a force protection tactic where military soldiers or units watch for enemy activity and provide cover fire on an objective as a friendly unit advances on that objective.

PAO—An acronym that stands for Public Affairs Office.

PB—An acronym that stands for Patrol Base.

PCS—An acronym that stands for Permanent Change of Station, used in the military when military personnel change assignments or stations and have to move to another location.

PIG—An acronym that stands for Professionally Instructed Gunman.

PIGs Tooth—A PIGs tooth is a 556 bullet, a smaller bullet you would shoot out of your M16 or M4, that hangs from 550 cord, an all-purpose cord. A PIGs tooth is what you get when you are in a Marine Corps Scout Sniper platoon but are not yet a school-trained sniper.

Pipe Hitters—A slang term used in the military to refer to people who are exceptional in what they do. It is also used to refer to "operators," which is a military term for a person who is highly trained to carry out special operations.

PKM—An improved 7.62mm PK (*Pulemyot Kalashnikova*) Soviet machine gun. Depending on where you look, the *M* either stands for "modernized" or "modified."

PMA—An acronym that stands for Positive Mental Attitude.

POG/Pogue—A slightly derogatory Marine Corps term that stands for "People other than grunts," but pronounced *pogue*.

Post Stander—Refers to a regular infantry Marine who stands watch at a post.

POW—An acronym that stands for Prisoners of War.

PSD—An acronym that stands for Personal Security Detachment.

PT—An acronym that stands for Physical Training. PT is used as a verb, "We are going to PT"; a noun, "PT was rough this morning"; and an adjective, "She was in PT gear," meaning she was in specific uniform clothes worn to exercise in.

PTSD—An acronym that stands for Posttraumatic Stress Disorder.

QRF—An acronym that stands for Quick Reaction Force.

Range Card—A range card is a hand-drawn document that is a graphical representation of the range distance to specific locations that is easily recognized by the shooter and observer and terrain in front of you. It lays out the assigned target reference points with the corresponding distance and azimuth to that location as well as the data you need to dial on the scope to hit a target at that location.

Ranger—A term for a United States Army Ranger who is a graduate of the Army's Ranger School. Rangers are part of the 75th Army Ranger Regiment, which is an elite airborne light infantry combat formation within the United States Army Special Operations Command (USASOC).

RCT—A military acronym that stands for Regimental Combat Team.

Recon—A term that stands for "reconnaissance."

Reconnaissance by fire or Recon by fire—Recon by fire is a warfare tactic, or wartime rule of engagement, where military forces are able to fire on likely enemy positions without actually seeing the enemy in order to provoke a reaction, such as firing back, in order to confirm enemy presence and positions.

RIP—An acronym that stands for Relieve in Place. This is when one military unit replaces another in a theater or area of operations (AO), providing the opportunity for the outgoing unit to train their backfill before departing the AO.

ROE—An acronym that stands for Rules of Engagement.

ROK—An acronym that stands for Republic of Korea.

RPG—An acronym that stands for Rocket Propelled Grenade, which is a shoulder-fired antitank weapon.

RPK—An acronym that stands for *Ruchnoy Pulemyot Kalashnikova*, a Soviet-designed handheld machine gun.

RSO—An acronym that stands for the Regional Security Officer. The officers are special agents from the State Department's Diplomatic Security Service who are responsible for all diplomatic security matters overseas, from threats of terrorist acts to protecting our classified information. They act as security advisors to U.S. ambassadors, and they are also responsible for keeping U.S. personnel and their families stationed overseas safe. They are also the liaison between the host country's law enforcement entities and conduct both criminal and personnel investigations.

R&S—An acronym that stands for Reconnaissance and Surveillance.

RUMINT—A slang term we use in the intelligence field that stands for "rumor intelligence," meaning uncorroborated information for which you have no idea of the veracity or legitimacy.

S-2—The S-2 refers to the to the military intelligence staff of a unit in the United States Marine Corps; G-2 refers to the to the military intelligence staff of a unit in the United States Army and higher-echelon units in the Marine Corps; N-2 refers to the to the military intelligence staff of a unit in the United States Navy; and J-2 refers to the military intelligence staff of a joint staff.

SAPI—An acronym that stands for Small Arms Protective Insert, which was a thick ballistic plate to stop bullets.

SASR—Special Application Scoped Rifle, pronounced *sass-ser*.

SAW—An acronym that stands for Squad Automatic Weapon.

SEAL—An acronym that stands for Sea, Air, Land; as in the United States Navy SEALs.

SERE—An acronym that stands for Survival Evasion, Resistance, and Escape. SERE is a training program that teaches how to evade capture, use survival skills, and the military code of conduct. SERE was established by the U.S. Air Force at the end of the Korean War (1950–1953). It was extended during the Vietnam War (1959–1975) to the U.S. Army, U.S. Navy, and U.S. Marine Corps for personnel considered to be at high risk of capture, such as special operations personnel and air crews.

SITREPS—An acronym that stands for Situation Reports.

SMAW—An acronym that stands for a Shoulder-Launched Multipurpose Assault Weapon.

SME—An acronym that stands for Subject Matter Expert.

SOCEX—An acronym that stands for Special Operations Capable Exercise Certifying.

SOCOM—An acronym that stands for Special Operations Command.

SOF—An acronym that stands for Special Operations Forces.

SOG—An acronym that stands for Sergeant of the Guard.

SOI—An acronym that stands for School of Infantry. There is an SOI West located in Camp Pendleton in California, and SOI East located at Camp Geiger, a satellite facility of Camp Lejeune in North Carolina.

SOP—An acronym that stands for Standard Operation Procedure.

SSBC—An acronym that stands for Scout Sniper Basic Course.

STA Platoon—STA is an acronym that stands for stands for Surveillance, Target, and Acquisition Platoon. It's pronounced *stay*. The STA Platoon in the Marine Corps works directly for the S-2 (intelligence section) and conducts reconnaissance, surveillance, and any other type of intelligence collection, but most importantly, the STA Platoon is the home of Marine Corps Scout Snipers.

SWAT—An acronym that stands for Special Weapons and Tactics.

Thin-Skinned Vehicle—A thin-skinned vehicle refers to a HMMWV, or any other vehicle, with no armor protecting it.

TTPs—An acronym that stands for tactics, techniques, and procedures.

Twentynine Palms—Refers to the Marine Corps Air Ground Combat Center (MCAGCC) located in Twentynine Palms, California.

UDP—An acronym that stands for Unit Deployment Program.

USLO—An acronym that stands for United States Liaison Office.

XM3—Short bolt-action 7.62mm/308 sniper rifle.

INDEX